THE 7 PILLARS
OF DIGITAL MARKETING

A Comprehensive Marketing System

Second Edition

By: Arman Rousta
Entrepreneur & CEO of Blueliner

Pillars of Marketing Series: Book 1

7 Pillars Digital Marketing Academy, LLC
Jersey City, NJ, USA

© 2015 7 Pillars Digital Marketing Academy, LLC / www.7pillarsdma.com

Edited by Allison Turza Bajger PhD.

Design, Cover and Illustrations: Eduard Balaž;
Icons: Damjan Dano (pages: 26, 27, 28, 29, 31, 33, 34, 35);
Exercises and Quick Tips: Allison Turza Bajger;
Contributor: Conor Dalton.

Printed and bound in the United States of America.

ISBN 978-0-9862365-1-8

To the valued clients and staff of Blueliner, without whom the 7 Pillars concept would not have been born and raised.

And to my dear son, Aydin, who (like this book) was also born in 2015, in the auspicious 7th month (July).

"Arman has created a new paradigm that guides brands and individuals to find their way in an increasingly complex digital world. 7 Pillars provides much needed structure and accountability to the field of marketing. This is a must read for entrepreneurs as well as everyone in corporate marketing departments."

⇨ **Rocco B. Commisso,** Chairman & CEO of Mediacom Communications Corp.

"Today, the world is overwhelmed with Digital, Social, Mobile Marketing tactics, tricks, tools and advice. Making it nearly impossible to figure out how to build a thoughtful plan of attack. Fortunately for all marketers and business owners, 7 Pillars has come along to help us all get a firm grasp on what matters most, how to prioritize and get a strong foundation for Digital Marketing success."

⇨ **Aaron Kahlow,** Founder, Online Marketing Institute
   🐦 *@aaronkahlow*

"In this era, more than ever we need a blueprint for digital marketing, and 7 Pillars is here to help marketers optimize every single aspect of their work. We needed a guide to think, plan and measure. At Web Congress, we think this book should be in every marketers hands."

⇨ **Ouali Benmeziane,** CEO, WebCongress, Inc
   💼 *linkedin.com/in/oualibenmeziane*

"7 Pillars is what agencies need to create winning strategies for their clients. It's based on years of practical experience that Arman has managed to convert into applied methodology. That is the key that makes it relevant and useful."

⇨ **Givi Topchishvili,** Founder & President of 9.8 Group

"I have personally witnessed the successful application of the 7 Pillars of Digital Marketing now twice, with major tourism and healthcare organizations in the Caribbean. This is not theoretical - it is a practical guide and toolbox, that deals skillfully with budgeting, ROI, branding and the various forms of lead generation and customer management that are required nowadays to remain competitive. I wish that we could have kept it under the radar longer; but at the same time, I am happy to see the marketing community receive this gift from Arman! This book will whet your appetite and leave you wanting more."

⇨ **Shomari Scott,** Marketing Director of Health City and formerly for Cayman Islands Department of Tourism

"Move over 6 Sigma! 7 Pillars is a scientific marketing methodology that makes sense of the vast and ever-changing ad tech industry. From Search to Social Media, this book is a fantastic introduction and foundation upon which one learns how to carve out their niche in the Internet ecosystem. 7 Pillars actually goes beyond marketing, as it applies well to business and management challenges too!"

⇨ **Matt McGowan,** Strategy @ Google and YouTube
   🔲 *linkedin.com/in/mcgowan*

"To navigate this exciting new digital world one needs a manual, a guide and a body of proven wisdom. The book you hold in your hands will stand the test of time and can be a key component of your digital marketing success for years to come."

⇨ **David Houle,** Futurist and Author of The Shift Age
   🐦 *@evolutionshift*

TABLE OF CONTENTS

The 7 Marketing Personality Types

MPT — Number Cruncher · Info Gatherer · Hunter · Farmer · Idea Person · Doer · Visionary

Prophet
of the pillars

The rare breed, Blue Samurai (Dimension 3, Level 7)
*Select Masters, Industry Leaders, Innovators and Guides

Foreword

It is a pleasure and an honor to write the foreword to this book. Over the past ten years I have seen the birth, evolution and now publication of it.

I first met Arman in 2001 when we worked together on a major project of his. I was immediately struck by his vision and entrepreneurial drive. A few years later, when he launched Blueliner Marketing, I immediately became a client as he and his associates seemed to be way ahead of anyone else in the digital marketing space. They started to do all the SEO work on my web site. This was in 2004 and 2005 before SEO became a term everyone knew. Today, when people ask me why I am consistently at or near the top of most search engine rankings as a futurist, I reference that I had smart people doing my SEO starting ten years ago.

In 2005, Arman told me that if I wanted to write a book I should start writing a blog. After asking what a blog was, I started one, www.evolutionshift.com. Arman even came up with the tagline for it that I use to this day: "A Future Look at Today". It was that blog that launched my career as a futurist. Eight years later, I am still writing it and people read it in numerous countries around the world.

So I speak from experience when I say that Arman and his 7 Pillars of Digital Marketing are part of my success.

I have seen this book evolve through ultimately successful development of all aspects of it in the marketplace. First there were three, then four, up to six and now finally seven pillars. Each one was diligently tested and refined as Arman created success after success for his clients. Once I achieved a level of success as a published author I began suggesting to Arman that he simply had to write a book about the 7 Pillars. That was years ago, so I am thrilled that he is finally bringing this wisdom to the market so that it can be shared with a wider audience.

Why is this both an important book and one that anyone who relies on digital marketing needs to read? We live and work in a new century and a new age, the Shift Age.

Forged in the fire
of marketing

Almost everything either has changed or will soon. Many old axioms of marketing are no longer valid, the speed of change is ever accelerating and the digital world is now redefining the physical or analog world. Disruptions occur almost daily. To navigate this exciting new digital world one needs a manual, a guide and a body of proven wisdom. Too many books today deal in superficial or purely executional terms about social media and online marketing so they are soon irrelevant. The book you hold in your hands will stand the test of time and can be a key component of your digital marketing success for years to come.

Jump right in and begin!

David Houle, Futurist
June 2015 – www.davidhoule.com
🐦 *@evolutionshift*

A Blueprint
for Marketing Excellence

Innovation Driven

Business Intelligence

Organic & Agile Workflow

Active Knowledge Sharing

Introduction to the 7 Pillars

The 7 Pillars of Digital Marketing™ is a comprehensive framework and a new paradigm for learning and mastering the ever evolving discipline of marketing. It provides a new prism through which to view strategy, budgeting, execution and analysis of the entire universe of integrated (digital and traditional) marketing ideas, tactics and techniques. 7 Pillars illuminates the entire Internet ecosystem – from Social Media to Website Analytics – and provides a practical methodology for understanding the full spectrum of digital marketing opportunities.

I was inspired to create 7 Pillars so that my staff and clients had access to a complete educational and organizational system, upon which we could build and apply marketing knowledge. We use it for the planning, execution and analysis of all types of marketing efforts.

7 Pillars is a practical and scientific approach to marketing, not some vague, jargon-laden theory. It has been forged in the fire of nearly 20 years of marketing trials and activity, on behalf of start-ups and Fortune 500 companies. It makes marketing accountable! The results – mistakes and successes alike – are brought forth into this all-encompassing, learnable methodology.

The beauty of 7 Pillars is that it brings every little detail – from a mobile app feature, to a specific search engine keyword – back to the whole. Marketing is a holistic, interconnected field that requires a framework to understand how everything fits together. Learning a specific tactic in a vacuum is counter-productive. The Pillars represent far more than specific tactics; they are overarching principles or energies that govern the marketing world.

This book introduces a complete, proven system for how to best find your place and thrive within the wide world of digital marketing. It is a hands-on guide that provides informative questions and valuable tools along the way.

Feel free to jump around, going straight to the areas which you are most interested in first. Each section and element, while part of a bigger system, can be learned on a standalone basis. However, I recommend that you read through the introduction pages and eventually touch on all elements of the program (i.e. all 7 Pillars, 7 Modes, 7 Angles, etc.) as this will give you a big picture comprehension of the marketing world. While reading different sections you can choose whatever path feels right, whether it is grasping ideas only or implementing an actual marketing campaign.

Remember, this is an **introductory** book to a vast framework that goes many layers deeper. Future complementary books will venture into various specific areas in greater detail, with books for each Pillar and Mode, as well as industry-specific best practice guides (i.e. 7 Pillars of Digital Marketing: Travel & Tourism Edition is the first specialized version in the works).

The 7 Pillars website **(www.7pillarsdigital.com)** also provides more in-depth information and resources, which can be accessed through the main site navigation or folder links (see below).

Pillar 1:	*7pillarsdigital.com/p1*
Traditional Pillar 2:	*7pillarsdigital.com/tp2*
Mode 5:	*7pillarsdigital.com/m5*
Angle 3:	*7pillarsdigital.com/a3*
Level 7:	*7pillarsdigital.com/l7*
Core Principle 4:	*7pillarsdigital.com/cp4*
Dimension 6:	*7pillarsdigital.com/d6*
Marketing Personality Type 1:	*7pillarsdigital.com/mpt1*

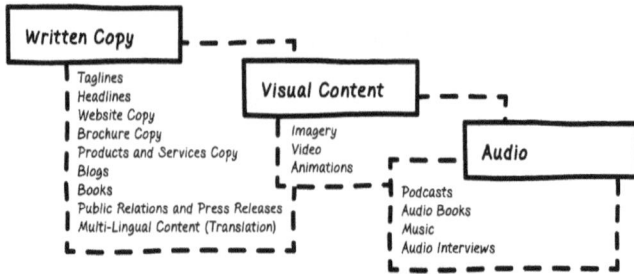

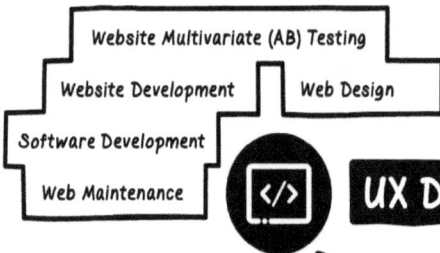

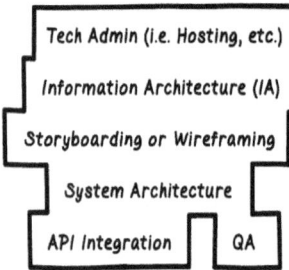

THE 7 PILLARS
OF DIGITAL MARKETING
TACTICS MAP

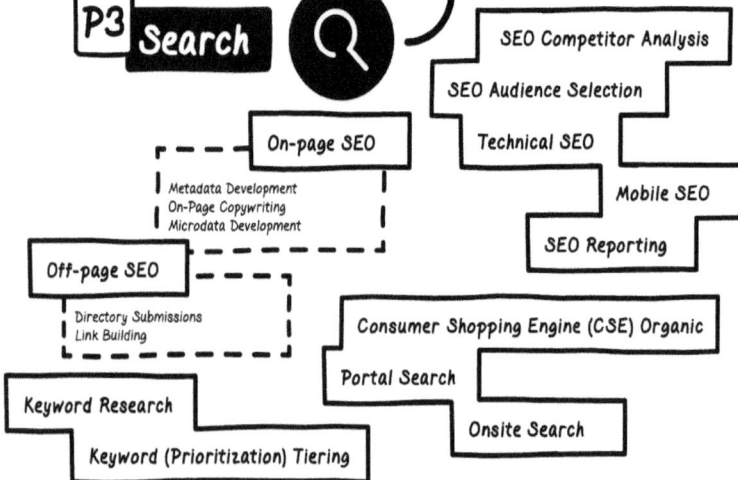

Content | P1

Written Copy
- Taglines
- Headlines
- Website Copy
- Brochure Copy
- Products and Services Copy
- Blogs
- Books
- Public Relations and Press Releases
- Multi-Lingual Content (Translation)

Visual Content
- Imagery
- Video
- Animations

Audio
- Podcasts
- Audio Books
- Music
- Audio Interviews

UX Design | P2

- Website Multivariate (AB) Testing
- Website Development
- Web Design
- Software Development
- Web Maintenance

- Tech Admin (i.e. Hosting, etc.)
- Information Architecture (IA)
- Storyboarding or Wireframing
- System Architecture
- API Integration
- QA

P3 | **Search**

- SEO Competitor Analysis
- SEO Audience Selection
- Technical SEO
- Mobile SEO
- SEO Reporting

On-page SEO
- Metadata Development
- On-Page Copywriting
- Microdata Development

Off-page SEO
- Directory Submissions
- Link Building

- Consumer Shopping Engine (CSE) Organic
- Portal Search
- Onsite Search
- Keyword Research
- Keyword (Prioritization) Tiering

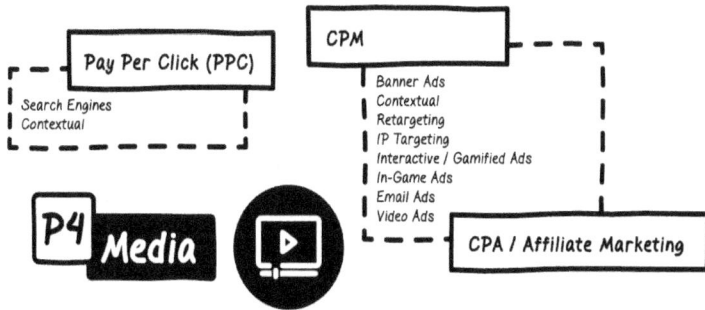

Pay Per Click (PPC)

- Search Engines
- Contextual

CPM

- Banner Ads
- Contextual
- Retargeting
- IP Targeting
- Interactive / Gamified Ads
- In-Game Ads
- Email Ads
- Video Ads

CPA / Affiliate Marketing

P4 Media

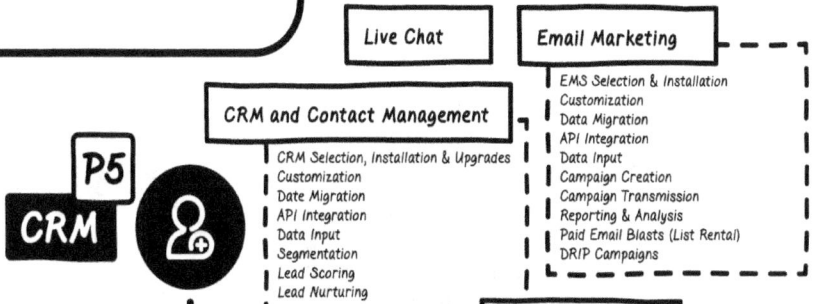

Live Chat

Email Marketing

- EMS Selection & Installation
- Customization
- Data Migration
- API Integration
- Data Input
- Campaign Creation
- Campaign Transmission
- Reporting & Analysis
- Paid Email Blasts (List Rental)
- DRIP Campaigns

CRM and Contact Management

- CRM Selection, Installation & Upgrades
- Customization
- Date Migration
- API Integration
- Data Input
- Segmentation
- Lead Scoring
- Lead Nurturing

P5 CRM

Analytics

- Web Analytics Selection & Installation
- Customization
- Segmentation
- Reporting

Customer Service

- Telephone Customer Service
- Email Customer Service
- Social Customer Service

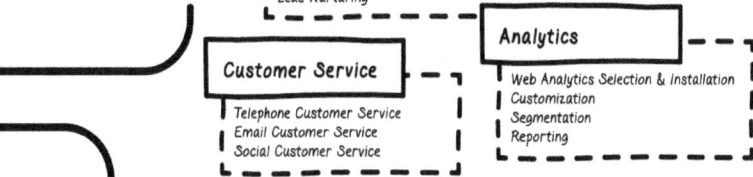

P6 Social

Organic Social

- Profile Creation & Management
- Original Posting (Images, Videos, Copy)
- Sharing and Commenting
- Reviewing, Rating, Liking
- Direct Messaging
- Group Subscriptions
- Event Postings & Management
- Live Event Productions

Paid Social

- Pay Per Click Ads
- CPM Ads
- Pay Per View Ads
- CPA Ads

Online PR

Social Gaming

Social Apps

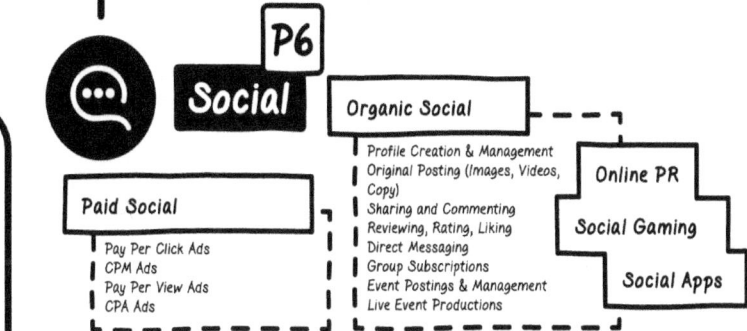

P7 Mobile

Mobile Advertising

- Mobile Ads
- In-App Ads
- Push Notification Ads

Mobile Apps

- Native Apps
- Hybrid Apps
- Web Apps

Mobile Websites

SMS Marketing

QR Codes

Proximity Marketing (i.e. Bluetooth)

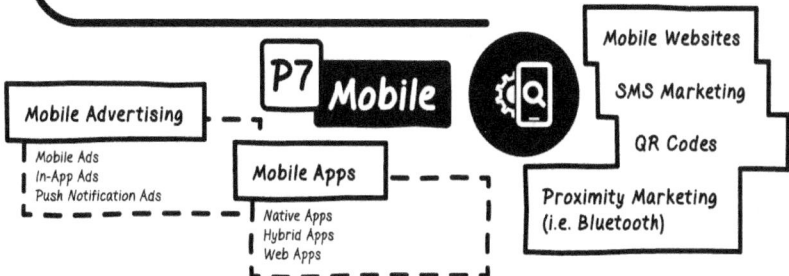

7 Core Principles

There are seven primary, defining characteristics that pervade the 7 Pillars methodology.

CP1

Time Mastery

Proactive time management, self-knowledge, awareness, and respect for time - one's own and others - is a cornerstone of 7 Pillars. A smart marketer **a)** recognizes that momentum and inspiration are impacting variables to productivity, and **b)** understands how to maximize a team's time by matching skill levels to priority projects and tasks.

CP2

Goal Driven

Productive and happy marketers are goal-oriented. Financial accountability is key but other Key Performance Indicators (KPIs), such as social impact, are also important. Therefore, every undertaking ought to begin and end with evaluating goals in mind. As the great Albert Einstein said, "If you want to live a happy life, tie it to a goal, not to people or objects."

CP3

Holistic & Integrated

7 Pillars is holistic on both marketing and global levels (2+2=5; seeking value creation and synergies amongst distinct tactics). We see how the 7 Pillars work together in sync to drive tangible results. Beyond pure campaign success, ethics really matter. W7 = Win-Win to the 7th Power and the impact on all seven levels must be weighed, including **1)** the Client **2)** the Agency **3)** the Client Staff **4)** the Agency Staff **5)** the Client's Customers **6)** Communities and **7)** the World. The scales have to be balanced. Each group needs to ask questions such as "How are we doing? Are we serving the overall team well?"

"The sum is greater than its parts."

"Innovators win. Copy cats are just playing catch-up."

Innovation Driven

Innovators win. Copy cats are just playing catch-up. 7 Pillars is about re-inventing and pushing the boundaries on best practices, which are changing faster than ever. You must try new things and evaluate problems from multiple angles in order to stay sharp and keep your problem-solving faculties fresh.

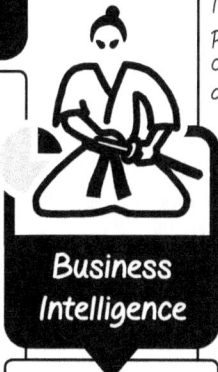

Business Intelligence

When in doubt, analyze and optimize everything. You can always learn something new by revisiting things with a clear mind and a fresh set of eyes. Business intelligence goes beyond looking at numbers, it is about generating valuable insights and actionable recommendations from trends and data.

Active Knowledge Sharing

I believe in the principles of crowdsourcing, open source and anti-fiefdom, all of which are open, collaborative systems. In today's world, the speed of change is faster than ever. Yesterday's knowledge is dead while tomorrow's is alive and kicking. The more we can bring together the collective consciousness of the more than 7 billion brains on the planet, the better off we will all be.

Organic & Agile Workflow

This system encourages adaptive adjustments. Karate great and teacher Bruce Lee said "Be like water, always flexible." High performers are focused but not fixated. They accommodate variations in work styles (Structure vs. Flexibility; Right vs. Left Brain synergy). Agile Project Management is the most effective way to tackle complex projects, which often have both evolving requirements and moving targets.

"Be like water, always flexible."

7 Dimensions: The Master Filtration System of Marketing Practices

There are 7 Dimensions within the 7 Pillars system, which act as a master filtration model within which we may organize our marketing knowledge and practices. Whether we are aware of it or not, at any given moment of our work life, we exist in one or more particular locations within each Dimension. Understanding the 7 Dimensions and our place within them improves our marketing awareness and performance, as well as our comprehension of team dynamics.

Dimension I: 7 PILLARS

The Pillars constitute the first and highest-level Dimension of the model and can be likened to planets in a solar system. The Pillars are the energy centers that govern all things in the marketing Universe. Everything ultimately flows through one or more of these central tenets.

Dimension II: 7 MODES

The Modes are almost equal to the Pillars in importance. While the Pillars are more high-level and conceptual, the Modes are planes of action. Each mode describes a different stage or modality through which various marketing actions are taken.

Dimension III: 7 ANGLES

Each angle refers to the different approaches, methods and job functions that we act through. Are you approaching a problem from a Designer's perspective? If so, you will likely apply the Creative Angle. The Angles combine with Levels (Dimension IV) to bring to life another key aspect and visual of the 7 Pillars Model - the Pyramids of Knowledge.

Dimension IV: 7 LEVELS

The Levels refer to the rank of expertise and skill within each Pillar, Mode and Angle "track" and can also be applied to the following two Dimensions, Markets and Industries. A 7 Pillars Assessment gives marketers a starting point from which they can gauge their true level. Karate Dojo analogies are used to depict the Levels by Belts - White, Yellow, Orange, Green, Brown, Black and Blue, the ultimate level reserved for masters of the game.

Dimension V: Markets

This Dimension includes all of the local and global exchanges which can be segmented geographically (i.e. Continent, Country, State, City), demographically (i.e. Income Level, Gender, Age, Ethnicity) and/or psychographically (i.e. user behaviour, special interests, etc.). This dimension has been turbo-charged by explosions of web connectivity, smartphone ubiquity and includes concepts such as multi-lingual websites and hyper-local marketing campaigns.

Dimension VI: Industries

Industries includes a discussion of major and sub-business divisions (i.e. Airlines as a sub-group of Travel & Tourism). Best practices and marketing tactics differ widely by industry, as do industry terminology and the regulatory environment.

Dimension VII: Time [Eras]

Digital Marketing best practices and tools are constantly changing. What was relevant yesterday, may not be applicable tomorrow. Dimension 7 highlights these historical and present day trends by parsing Digital Marketing into Eras, most broadly; the Past, Present and Future. You can also utilize this Dimension to map your career history, set goals for upcoming periods and gain comprehension on how many hours are required to build new skill sets, allowing you to maximize your potential.

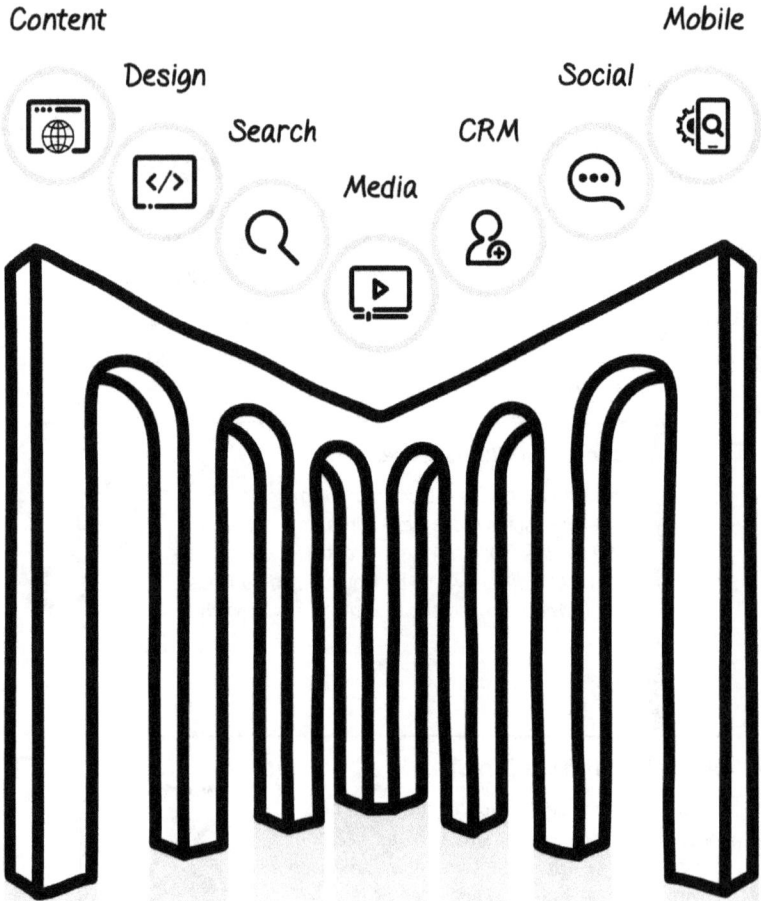

The **7** Pillars
of Digital Marketing
...Sustain Digital Life

Content

Mobile

Design

Social

Search

CRM

Media

Encapsulating the entire Internet Ecosystem

The 7 Pillars of Digital Marketing

Terminology-wise, in addition to being the name of the overall system, "7 Pillars" also represents the first (and broadest of seven) Dimension of the system.

For the most part, when the term is used throughout the book, the context should make it clear as to which "7 Pillars" is being referenced. Where it may not be clear, I sometimes add a word to leave no room for error (e.g. "the 7 Pillars system" or "the 7 Pillars (D1)" referring to the first Dimension of the model).

The 7 Pillars (D1) encapsulate the whole Internet Universe, distilling it down into these vital categories that literally sustain "digital life." The Pillars (see image to the left) are broad and all-encompassing, and have within them, many levels of sub-specialties, marketing tactics, associated technology platforms and strategies. The purpose of this book is to give a high-level overview of this Universe and will not provide a great level of detail. However, more detail is provided on the website/additional training materials.

I recommend that marketers and entrepreneurs pick one or at most 2 Pillars as their Major, as you did in college. You should then ask yourself where do you want to develop your expertise? The answer to this question requires the selection of 2-3 Minors, which will serve as strategic complements to your Major and related goals.

The same exercise of picking 1 Major and 2 Minors will also be necessary for Dimensions 2 (Modes), 4 (Angles), and in more advanced cases, 5 (Markets) and 6 (Industries). We will discuss more on this later.

Beyond your Major(s), true to the holistic and harmonious nature of this system, it is imperative to learn at least the basics across all 7 Pillars in order to be an effective marketer.

Pillar I [P1]: Content

For Traditional and Digital Marketing alike, content is still (and always has been) King! Content is the life-blood of all marketing, which is particularly apparent online. After all, the entire web is comprised of searchable content. If it weren't for content, Search Engines would be non-existent, as would Social Networks.

Content is a prominent Pillar and works through the other Pillars in a more interdependent manner than any other. Content covers all forms of copywriting, including website, blog, social media and online ad copy. Photography (both stock and original) is also an important form of content for website properties, as video assets are for digital usage. So we have *1)* Text, **2)** Audio, **3)** Video and **4)** Graphical forms of Content.

There is all kinds of buzz nowadays about Content Marketing and Inbound Marketing, as if these were new marketing concepts. They are not. The industry is now just taking a different spin and systematic approach to Content, having realized how vital it is to plan and organize successful marketing campaigns.

Every single day, a new record is set for the amount of Content that is created and stored in "the Cloud" and organized by Search Engines like Google – representing an ever-expanding digital Universe. It really is truly mind-blowing. The guidance for the smart 7 Pillars marketer is to carve out his or her own niche and become some type of "Content Creator", be it as an individual or on behalf of a company.

As is the case in the Traditional Pillar of Branding, Content is a key signifier of a company. If Branding is a company's personality, Content is certainly its voice.

Pillar 2 [P2]: Design

If Content is King, User Experience (UX) Design is Queen. How well they come together determines, to a large part, the quality of a brand's expression.

I wrestle with whether to call this Pillar "Design" or "UX" since the argument can be made either way that one entails the other. Design is a broader term and more people can relate to it, so we'll go with that as the official one word Pillar name. However, as far as I'm concerned, they are interchangeable.

This Pillar covers all aspects of digital UX, including Web Development, App Development, Web Design and even Web Hosting & Maintenance. Every element on every page of a website calls for well thought-out UX, including creative assets, like banner ads, forms, calls to action and header graphics. Heavy interaction with other Pillars is shown here, as these marketing assets take direction from Design's parallel Traditional Pillar 2 (Branding) and utilize Pillar 1 (Content).

UX, more so than other digital Pillars, exists in the traditional, non-digital world as well. UX is in everything, from product design to architecture to even marketing brochures. Feng Shui is an example of UX in the physical realm, in that it involves organizing furniture and space in a way that optimizes the experience of those who live in or visit that space.

There are many types of designers (i.e. Graphical Artists, Information Architects, Iconographers, Animators etc.) in this broad ecosystem. I also include technical folks in this as well, because they greatly impact UX. The way a web or mobile page comes to life, through different page states and interactive elements, depends largely on how intelligently the UX is coded by programmers.

Pillar 3 [P3]: Search

Search highlights a quantum leap that the Internet has enabled marketers and people in general to enjoy. Thanks to the power of this mighty Pillar, finding what one seeks and much more has never been so effortless. Mastery of Search has yielded billions of dollars in revenue for many entrepreneurs and online companies. Meanwhile, our collective dependency on "The Search Gods" (a.k.a. Google) has everyone scrambling to crack the code, spawning new industries, namely Search Engine Optimization (SEO).

The Search Pillar entails more than just Search Engines, it also corresponds to the principles of Search all over the web, such as insite search (i.e. the Search function within each website), product search (i.e. within sites like Amazon.com, Staples.com and Zappos.com), and essentially the Search for anything within specific niche sites (i.e. Real Estate, Vacations, etc.).

Includes:

Insite search (i.e. the Search function within each website), product search (i.e. within sites like Amazon.com, Staples.com and Zappos.com); Search for anything within specific niche sites (i.e. Real Estate, Vacations, etc).

Best practices in Search change quite frequently, with Google's Panda updates causing many a marketer to lose sleep over his or her job security. The general advice that I give is that all SEO evolution is geared towards highlighting more useful, interesting and engaging content for end users. Therefore, in essence, SEO is all about Content and UX (Pillars 1 and 2) and, highlighting how holistic the marketing success model truly is. Just dumping keywords frequently into a web page does not work the same way it used to and in fact, nowadays it can even get your website penalized. Focus on creating truly great Content that provides value and differentiates you in the marketplace. Focus on making the user experience intuitive and you will be a step ahead of most in the Search space.

Pillar 4 [P4]:   Media

Pillar 4 comprises all forms of Online Advertising, essentially any paid media placement including banner ads, PPC ads (Pay Per Click), endorsements, sponsored emails and Social Media advertising. This Pillar's core concept of paid media is present in various forms across several other Pillars (i.e. Social, CRM, Search etc.) again highlighting the interconnectedness of this system.

Includes:

Banner ads; PPC (Pay Per Click) ads; Endorsements; Sponsored emails and also ads within social networks.

Paid Media, as opposed to Earned Media (Organic Social Media and SEO) and Owned Media (Publishers who own the content and advertising channels), is the most popular form of Digital Marketing and is also where the most money is spent. Google is a mega company because of its success in becoming the pre-eminent channel for Paid Media through its PPC system, Google Adwords.

It is quite easy to do it yourself and get started with Online Advertising without much prior experience. This makes it very accessible, yet also very easy to lose money fast if you don't know what you're doing, much like online trading.

There are different ways to pay for Online Media. This includes PPC, CPA (Cost Per Acquisition) or rather Affiliate Marketing, and display or banner CPM (Cost Per Impression), whereby you pay for placements on various advertising networks without any guarantee of how many people will actually click your ads.

For agencies and companies of all sizes, having excellent Digital Media strategists is of great importance because they can make or break your whole marketing budget. For success, it is vital to utilize the right channels and target the best audiences with an effective message, all while continuously optimizing your campaign.

Superior CRM Leads to...

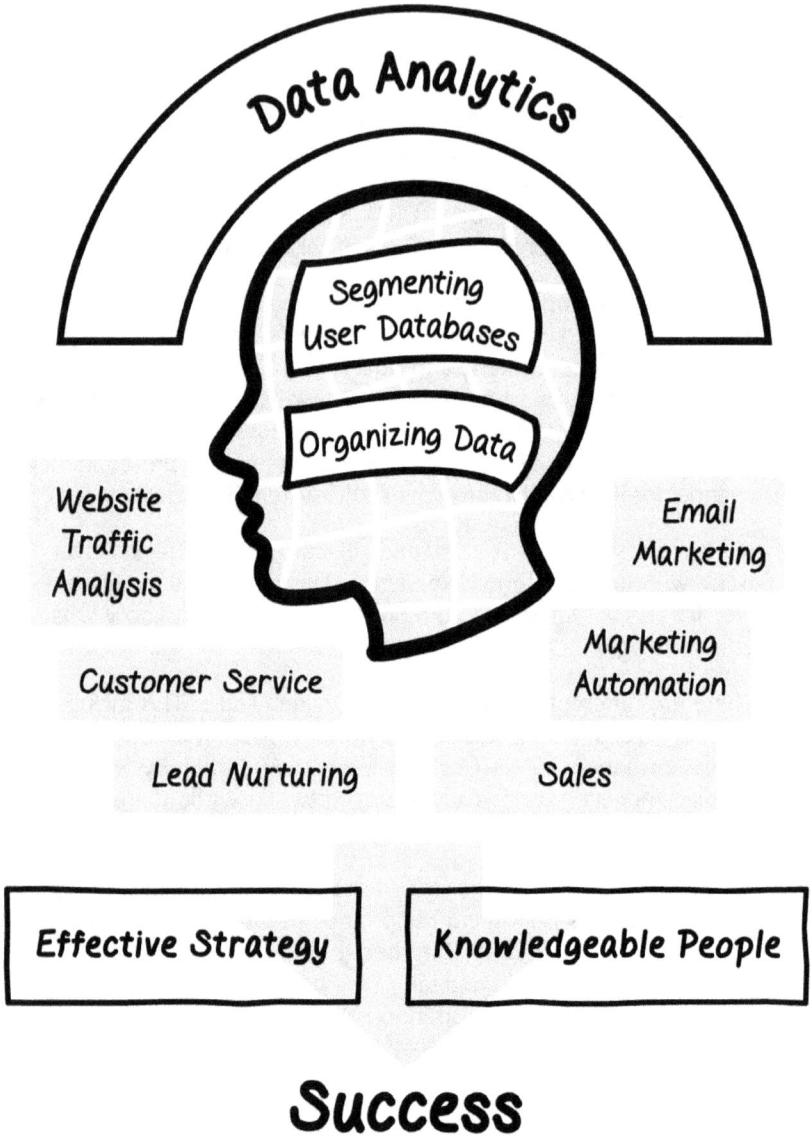

Data Analytics

Segmenting User Databases

Organizing Data

Website Traffic Analysis

Email Marketing

Customer Service

Marketing Automation

Lead Nurturing

Sales

Effective Strategy

Knowledgeable People

Success

Pillar 5 [P5]: CRM

Customer Relationship Management (CRM), in the context of the 7 Pillars model, refers to all forms of customer or lead interaction and the associated tools that organizations use to manage their contact data. Segmenting user databases by various demographics and characteristics is a core CRM function. Email Marketing, to either prospective or existing customers, is another key CRM tactic. As of late, there is a big trend towards Marketing Automation and Lead Nurturing, both of which fall under the Pillar of CRM. CRM is a very close cousin of its Traditional Marketing counterpart, Sales. Customer Service is also an aspect of CRM and one that is often undervalued.

Includes: Email Marketing and EMS SaaS tools like Mailchimp, Web Analytics, CRM software like Salesforce and SugarCRM, Marketing Automation tools like Marketo.

In order to track and organize key CRM data, we use tools like Google Analytics (Web data insights and reporting tool), Salesforce (a leading CRM contact database system) and Mailchimp (a popular Email Marketing Software or Solution [EMS]). Most CRM tools at present are Software as a Service (SaaS) where data is stored in the Cloud and accessed through websites and mobile apps. Mobile CRM strategies, like SMS marketing, are also on the rise.

CRM is not generally a lead generating Pillar, which allows it to be undervalued very easily. Most small businesses do not have effective CRM solutions in place that can deal with the workflow of data that is produced as potential customers start interacting with them. The good news is that, with proper training and attention, there is a goldmine of opportunities that an effective CRM strategy and execution can uncover. Like all of the Pillars, effective strategy will require good, knowledgeable people, who know how to segment customers, manage preferences and communicate effectively to different customer needs.

Social Media KPIs
Measuring Engagement

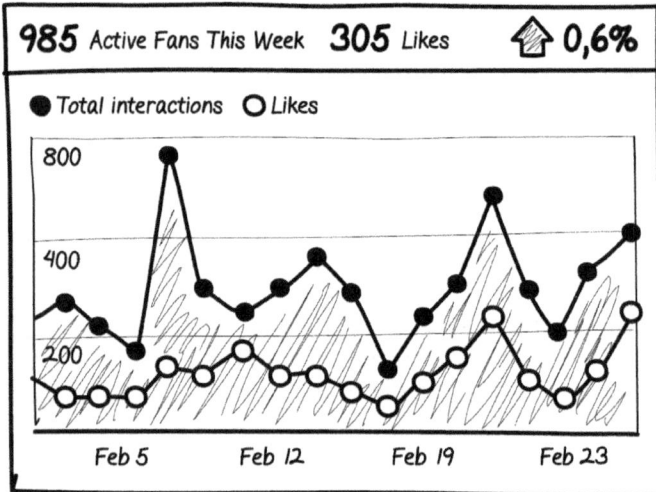

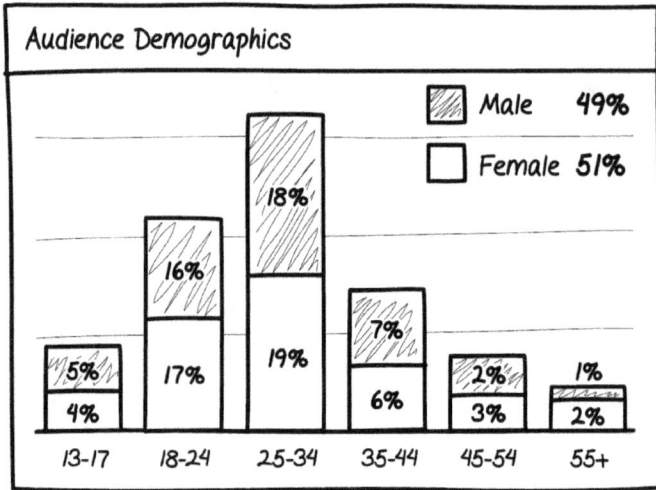

985 Active Fans This Week   **305** Likes   ⬆ **0,6%**

● Total interactions   ○ Likes

800			
400			
200			

Feb 5   Feb 12   Feb 19   Feb 23

Audience Demographics

▨ Male   49%
☐ Female   51%

	13-17	18-24	25-34	35-44	45-54	55+
Male	5%	16%	18%	7%	2%	1%
Female	4%	17%	19%	6%	3%	2%

Pillar 6 [P6]: **Social**

Since Facebook's ascension between 2005-2008, Social Media has become the most sought after, discussed and now utilized Pillar in the whole world of marketing. Everyone who is online essentially participates in Social Media through some form or another, presenting a great opportunity for marketers.

Pillar 6 includes all forms of organic Social Media activity. This includes communications within all social networks (i.e. Facebook, Twitter, LinkedIn, Google+, Instagram, Snapchat and the plethora of others), relationship building with prospective customers and industry influencers, as well as content distribution. Online PR, an extension of Traditional PR, falls under Pillar 6 as well since it is a form of Social Media, in a sense.

The ROI on Social is typically a combination of metrics, beyond merely financial goals. Some pivotal KPIs for this Pillar include general awareness, relationship development, influence, retention, referrals and overall engagement. You may notice that several of these KPIs relate closely to the highly interrelated Pillar 5 (CRM).

Includes:

Facebook;
Twitter;
LinkedIn;
Google+;
Snapchat.

Key KPIs:

General awareness;
Relationship development;
Influence;
Retention;
Referrals and overall engagement.

Statistics on Social will continue to break new boundaries for the foreseeable future, as the following Pillar 7 (Mobile) is making Social Media globally ubiquitous. The way to effectively engage Pillar 6 involves thoughtful and focused strategy, rather than trying to be everywhere and indiscriminately blast out messages and promotions. This is relevant for both personal and professional networking. Almost all of the Pillars come into play for effective Social Media, including a strong Content (P1) Marketing plan.

Pillar 7 [P7]: Mobile

Includes:

GPS;
Accelerometer;
In-app
advertising;
Phone-taken
images and
videos.

By 2020, there is no doubt that there will be at least one mobile device for each person on the planet, meaning more citizens will have instant access to the Internet and a handheld payment mechanism. Mobile represents the largest frontier of connectivity and the broadest scale opportunity that the world has ever known, making Pillar 7 the final, outermost tenet. The implications for people, as well as businesses, are vast and generally, aside from side effects like radiation and accessibility issues, very positive.

In 7 Pillars, Mobile covers everything from mobile apps to mobile websites and mobile advertising. It is almost big enough to require its own distinct category from the whole of Digital Marketing. More so than any other Pillar, Mobile is in the center and all other Pillars can be viewed through this lens. Here is a quick example, looking at things from a Mobile perspective:

Exercise:

Using the 7 Pillars framework, create an effective mobile in-app advertising campaign for your company, based on a hypothetical budget of $50,000 over 3 months. Consider the following questions to help guide your thinking:

1) Describe the skills of the person you will assign to lead the campaign execution? (Mode 4)

2) What content and calls to action will you include in the message? (Pillar 1)

3) How will you make the user experience engaging and non-intrusive? (Pillar 2)

4) What forms of online advertising will you utilize (i.e. PPC, CPM, Affiliate) (Pillar 4)

P1. Content

Localized content is more important due to the mobility factor. Concise content is also required for smaller screens.

P2. UX

Screen effects and phone tech capabilities including GPS and accelerometer, advance new UX potential and options.

P3. Search

Local search is a given. Search results are condensed and Click to Call takes on a new level of significance.

Seeing All Pillars Through the Eyes of One

(P7. Mobile)

P4. Media

Geo-targeted ads, including in-app advertising, allows for new opportunities to acquire customers.

P5. CRM

Within 2 years, more people will read emails on their phones than desktop, creating another targeting opportunity for businesses.

P6. Social

Social is Mobile's best friend, considering how much Social Media comes from phone-taken images and videos.

How does Pillar 1 (Content)
relate to all the others?

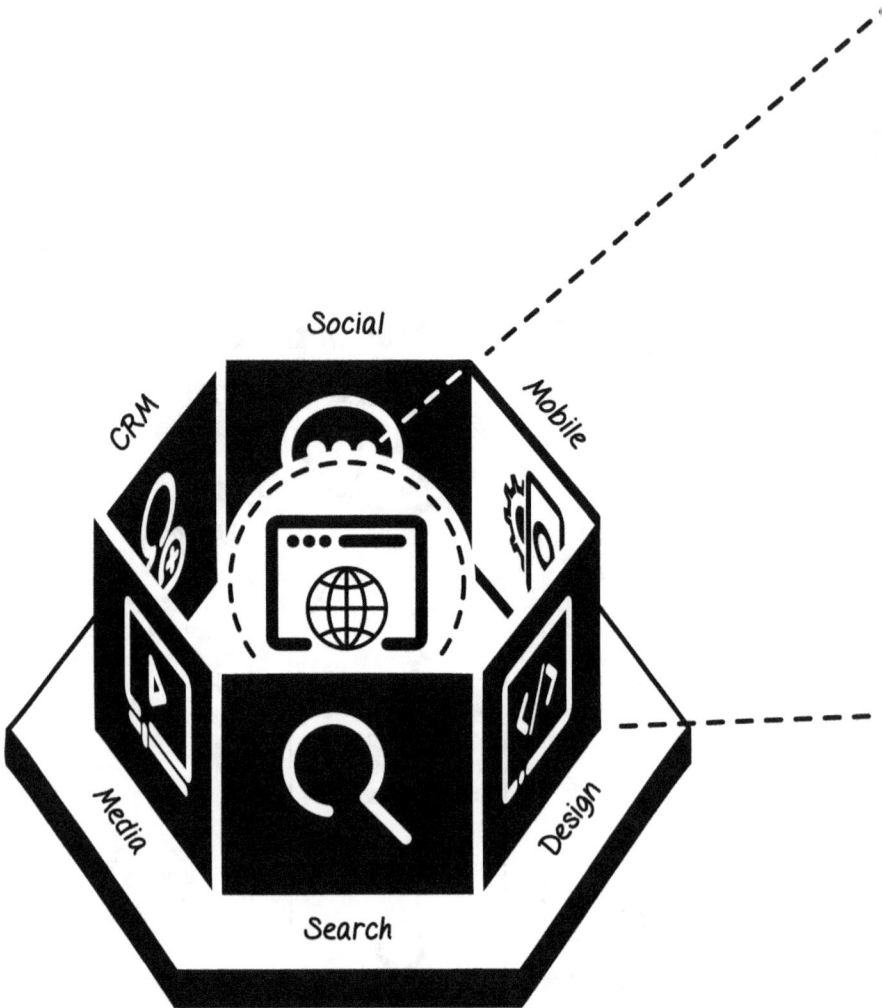

Content   Mobile

Exercise

Review each Pillar and brainstorm how Pillar 1 (Content) relates to each other Pillar. Specifically, make a list of 3 different ways in which Pillar 1 influences other Pillars and vice versa, as it relates to your company or a new business idea. Ask the following questions:

1) How well does the current website Content (P1) jive with the current Design (P2)?

2) How does your website Content (P1) drive Search (P3) and Social (P6) outcomes?

3) What types of Content (P1) drive the most sales for your main target audience in your Mobile (P7) Advertising (P4) campaigns? (HINT: Consider using CRM (P5) tools like Google Analytics and Facebook Pixels to track this data).

Never Forget Our Roots:
Traditional Marketing (Still) Matters!

The 7 Pillars of Traditional Marketing

It is very important to consider offline or Traditional Marketing (TM) theory and tactics as part of the overall 7 Pillars framework. Therein lie the roots of the Marketing field.

Comprehending Traditional Marketing requires a sense for the history of Marketing. Marketing Communications as an industry has gone through a number of Eras (see chapter discussion on Dimension 7). Marketing has been around in some form or another since essentially the beginning of time. The term – "Communications" – started as far back as the ancient Egyptians, who used hieroglyphic symbols to tell stories and record important data. Ever since human beings could speak, they gathered to hear clan leaders discuss new ideas or traveling merchants pitch their products. Town bazaars and the old Silk Road of the Middle East and Asia reflect the oldest forms of Traditional Pillars 5 (Sales) and 6 (Events).

Since the modern era's launch of mass communications (i.e. Television, Radio and Newspapers), Traditional Marketing has evolved into the dominant method of psychological warfare – the battle for influence of the mind and corresponding human behavior. The methods and channels through which companies and marketers seek to influence humanity have no end. People are unconsciously hooked to the marketing machine and its most popular messages. Big companies with big budgets, and backed by big banks, have the most ammunition and therefore, typically win the game. While this influence has only increased with the advent and explosive growth of the Internet, the playing field has also leveled a bit, allowing startups and smaller companies more of a chance to compete. Consumers also have more tools through which they can exert their own influence, marketing preferences (i.e. Do Not Call lists, SPAM laws) and sense of choice.

Like any true holistic approach, we do not simply draw a line in the sand and say "everything on this side is digital and the other side is traditional." This is a classic mistake that some agencies and executives make, leading to inefficiencies, unnecessary competition between factions and frequent restructuring of marketing departments. While sensible divisions can be made, it's necessary to put more emphasis on the numerous connection points – on

D1 TM

Integrated Marketing
Mirroring of the Pillars

Digital Pillars   Traditional Pillars

Digital	Traditional
Content	
Design	Branding
Advertising	
Search	Events
CRM	Sales
Social	PR
Mobile	Direct

Integrated Marketing – which if strategized effectively, can bring about unexpected benefits and marketing success to companies.

At one point, there was a time where digital marketing had to prove itself worthy of getting a piece of the marketing budget. However, in today's marketing world everything is integrated into digital. With that being said, the pendulum has unfortunately now swung too far in the opposite direction. Too many practitioners have declared traditional media "dead" and aren't paying attention to some very important facets of marketing that are fundamentally traditional in origin and nature.

One would assume that the 7 Digital and 7 Traditional Pillars combine to make 14 Pillars. However, the two Pillar systems actually combine to make up the 12 Pillars of Integrated Marketing (7 + 7 = 12) because two Pillars on each "side" (Content and Advertising) combine into one.

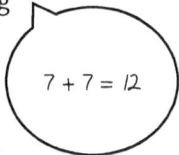

$7 + 7 = 12$

In some sense, Traditional Marketing now has to share the stage with its equally powerful Digital counterpart. In another sense, Traditional has become more important than ever due to the fact that its channels can be amplified and given nearly eternal life through digital add-ons and integration. Consider a Traditional TV ad with a Twitter hashtag and call to action; this ad now has an extended life and influence beyond the brand awareness created by the 30 second spot.

In this Chapter, we briefly outline the 7 Pillars of TM, with a particular emphasis on how they both differ from and relate to DM. Even the most technology focused digital natives can benefit professionally and sharpen their skill sets by comprehending the fundamentals of TM. Taking a broader view, we also see how TM paved the way for DM, giving us a language and foundation from which DM could be developed.

In conceptualizing the 7 Pillars system, I recognized how important it was to give weight to and properly integrate traditional marketing (TM) concepts into this model. **The 7 Pillars of Traditional Marketing (tP1-tP7)** are outlined below.

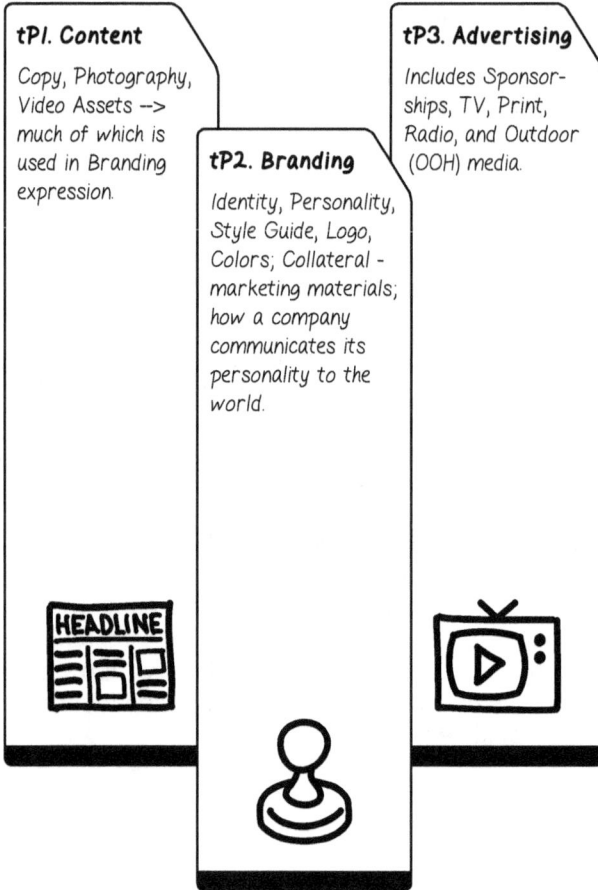

tP1. Content

Copy, Photography, Video Assets --> much of which is used in Branding expression.

tP2. Branding

Identity, Personality, Style Guide, Logo, Colors; Collateral - marketing materials; how a company communicates its personality to the world.

tP3. Advertising

Includes Sponsor-ships, TV, Print, Radio, and Outdoor (OOH) media.

tP4. PR

Public Relations, "earned" media, editorial placements; includes endorsements --> Online PR & Social Media are strongly connected to this area.

tP5. Sales

Includes overall Sales efforts, such as Customer Service, telemarketing, business development, cold calling and presentations. Also includes Point of Sale marketing, such as merchandising, end cap displays and in-store customer support.

tP6. Events

Trade shows, conferences, corporate events, fund-raisers, grass roots, street marketing, guerilla, flash mobs, performances, concerts, etc.

tP7. Direct (Response, DR)

Infomercials, Direct Mail, DRTV.

Content is the Core
of Your Brand's Personality

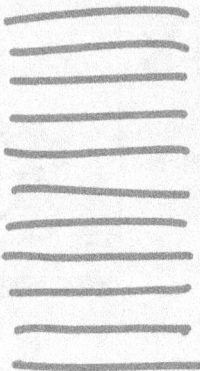

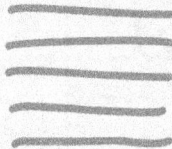
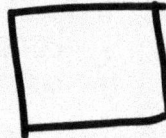

Traditional Pillar I [tP1]:

Content

While the Pillars are not necessarily numbered by importance, Content is Pillar #1 – in both Traditional and Digital – for good reason. High quality Content is what enables traditional media companies to garner billions of dollars in advertising. People want to consume *good* content and are willing to watch, read or listen to ads that provide this to them.

The concept of Owned Media originates from this Pillar as writers, producers, directors, investors, actors, athletes and celebrities of all kinds aspire to create iconic Content (tP1) and Brands (tP2) in order to attract big dollar Advertising (tP3). This 1-2-3 punch is the defining characteristic of Traditional Marketing, which has been effectively replicated in the Digital sphere.

> *Includes*:
> Creative writing (ie. books, screenplays, editorials); Promotional copywriting; Art; Photography (stock and original).

Traditional Content covers creative writing (i.e. books, screenplays and editorials), promotional copywriting, art, photography (stock and original) for traditional Advertising, radio shows, television shows, movies, sports, music and other forms of live entertainment. In many ways, tP1 is the purest form of creative and artistic expression in the entire 7 Pillars model. Much of it is produced for its own sake, more so than as a marketing vehicle. In fact, the marketing industry has been built and shaped around this creative energy center.

Certain types of Content succeed more than others, especially in Western culture. If the context is more advertising friendly, then odds of financial success are much higher. An example of this can be seen with American Football, where 50% of a 3-hour game shows commercials versus Soccer, where only 10% of a 2-hour game shows commercials. There is no better strategy in marketing than to create unique and captivating Content, around which memorable Branding and measurable Advertising models can be constructed. That being said, at the same time there is also nothing more difficult in marketing and therein lies the challenge.

Traditional Pillar 2 [tP2]:

Branding

Includes:

Features;
Names; Symbols;
Designs;
Language;
Fonts; Attitudes;
Culture
and overall
personality
associated with a
particular entity.

The Traditional Pillar 2 of Branding pervades all corners of Marketing, including Digital. It is one of the most misunderstood and simultaneously important areas of marketing to "get right" in order to achieve success. Some people view Branding as a straightforward creative process; design a logo, add some taglines and you're done. While these are indeed elements of Branding, they represent only a small part of the picture.

The word "brand" derives from the Old Norse word "brandr" meaning "to burn", recalling the practice of producers burning their mark (or brand) onto their products. Companies started branding their products as far back as the Vedic period in India (1100 BC). Since the industrial revolution, in addition to mass production brand labeling, companies began ascribing qualities to their products in order to target certain demographics.

Brands have become more refined, segmented and sophisticated over the years, as evidenced by the value Wall Street puts on them as an intangible asset on company balance sheets. There is more to it than having a unique and globally recognized logo that makes Coca-Cola an iconic and multi-billion dollar brand. The psychological and emotional qualities that companies spend billions of advertising dollars on elevate such brands.

Branding entails a multitude of factors including the unique and differentiating features, names, symbols, designs, language, fonts, attitudes, culture and overall personality associated with a particular entity. Good Branding helps answer the question, "What is your USP?" (Unique Selling Proposition), and develops Brand awareness within a particular target audience. In the 7 Pillars model, strong Branding requires an authentic and creative expression of an organization's deepest values, whereby the brand's promise is closely aligned with its actual deliverables.

Traditional Pillar 3 [tP3]:

Advertising

Advertising is Pillar 3 in the Traditional sphere and Pillar 4 in Digital. Traditional Advertising (TA) includes television, print, radio and Out of Home (OOH) advertising (i.e. outdoor billboards, bus signage, etc.) In spite of a strong movement towards Online Advertising, TA is far from dead, and in fact as of 2015, still gets a significantly larger slice of the media budget pie. tP3 is here to stay, and is undergoing a renaissance of its own.

> **Includes:**
>
> Television; Print; Radio and Out of Home (OOH) advertising (i.e. outdoor billboards, bus signage, etc).

During the conceptual and planning stages of a marketing campaign (i.e. Modes 1 Brainstorming, Mode 2 Budgeting and Mode 3 Strategy), typically Advertisement creation and execution is the biggest marketing investment under consideration. This can be daunting and put a lot of pressure on the creative and media departments to come up with killer campaigns that generate significant buzz. The right percentage of tP3 in a marketing plan can vary from 0% to 80%, depending on the overall objectives, size of the company, market opportunity and other variables. For a startup with $10,000 per month to spend on marketing, Blueliner generally wouldn't even look at Traditional Advertising. However, there are exceptions especially in the B2B marketing space, where tP3 tends to cost less and be targeted towards key decision makers.

Most marketers know the famous quote by John Wanamaker, "Half the money I spend on advertising is wasted; the trouble is I don't know which half." That shouldn't happen anymore. The level at which we can track online marketing provides this medium with a real and major advantage over traditional media. It has also brought about a new wave of accountability and models that enable marketers to better track traditional channels, like TV and print as well. Web TV is helping, as are cloud-based CRM systems, Social Media hashtags and unique URLs (as an example, something like www.xyzco.com/TV-offer).

Traditional Pillar 4 [tP4]:
Public Relations

Public Relations (PR) is almost a mirror image of its Digital counterpart, Social Media. Both of these monumentally important Pillars have to do with some type of earned media promotion, awareness building and reputation management.

What is PR exactly? In short, it is the management of nonpaid, strategic communications between an entity and its target market(s) or the public at large. I always like to call it a "wildcard marketing strategy" because its results can fluctuate greatly. Effective PR for the right individuals or companies, who have the right story to tell, can generate unbelievable ROI results and a viral impact beyond everyone's expectations. PR certainly doesn't happen over-night and it is not 100% necessary to engage in for every company.

PR generates materials for distribution to members of the media/press, press release writing, newsletters, speech writing, speaking engagements, press conferences, video and audio news releases (VNRs/ANRs) and other types of publicity events.

PR also has its own strong extension into Digital called Interactive or Online PR, which is closely related to but not exactly the same as Social Media. Interactive PR is simply the pitching and promoting of editorial content through online publications (i.e. Huffington Post, CNN.com, etc.) Social Media has more to do with organic relationships and groups on social networks such as Facebook and Twitter. Nowadays, every news organization has both online and offline distribution, which either share or split editorial teams. Quality PR marketers work hard to segment and prioritize media contacts and blend their outreach to access the broadest possible audience across as many different media sources as possible.

Traditional Pillar 5 [tP5]:

Sales

No organization survives without Sales because it forges a company's relationship with its customers. It is a close cousin of Digital Pillar counterpart; CRM, because both focus on customer development and management.

Sales covers a broader array of tasks and specialty areas than what you might imagine. For example, in-store merchandising (i.e. how products are presented and displayed) is a Sales function, which also relates heavily to Branding (tP2). However, this is only the first step of the Sales process. Once a startup company convinces mass merchant buyers to place their new innovation in retail stores, the company then has to develop a Point of Sale (POS) strategy that includes ways to educate store patrons and call attention to the product amidst a sea of other brands. Even with top-notch branding, products rarely, if ever, sell themselves.

Includes:

Networking;
Telemarketing;
Cold Calling;
In-Store
Merchandising;
Point of Sale
(POS) Strategy;
Customer
Service; Pitch
Meeting &
Presentation
Development;
Referral
Strategies.

Let's settle this once and for all. Sales is part of the big picture Marketing process and cannot be siloed. It has earned a spot in the 12 Pillars of Integrated Marketing model (remember, Traditional + Digital = Integrated) because it is inextricably linked to every other Pillar.

Sales oriented people have been some of the greatest beneficiaries of the digital revolution due to the enormous amount of data, tools and business intelligence tools that make their jobs easier. This Traditional Pillar has only been strengthened and amplified by the Internet. The following exercise will demonstrate this.

Traditional Pillar 6 [tP6]:

Event Marketing

Includes:

Trade shows;
Conferences;
Seminars;
Street fairs;
Concerts;
Performances;
Flash mobs and
other forms of
guerilla or grass
roots marketing.

Event Marketing is any pre-planned, live promotional or educational event, appearance or program. This includes trade shows, conferences, seminars, street fairs, concerts, performances, flash mobs and other forms of guerilla or grass roots marketing. Naturally, digital tech has greatly augmented the reach and impact of Event Marketing. This includes supporting features like mobile location-based promotions, live streaming, real-time social media imagery, web product demos, collaborative consumption (i.e. when a group of friends watches an event "together" from separate locations) and webinars.

I have a tremendous respect for Event Marketing because it is the most effective and "old school" marketing method of bringing people face to face. Event Marketing, in many ways, is a visceral extension of Sales, Branding and Advertising. The opportunity to stand in front of prospective customers in a staged environment that shows your offerings in the best light is golden. There is a huge ecosystem in this industry, including conferences that teach best practices and trends.

As with most Pillars, the "right" budget for Events depends on the company in question, as well as the industry, objectives, target audience, overall marketing budget and many other variables. If you are dealing with a visual product line (i.e. something that is nice to look at, touch or experience in person) then trade shows should at least be considered. If you need to get in front of buyers that are hard to reach through cold-calling or email, then this Pillar could be an effective channel for you, assuming those buyers are likely to frequent the respective show circuit. Event Production, a function within tP6, takes a lot of time, energy and a special expertise. Firms must budget and plan well for the whole exercise of pre-show, onsite and post-show marketing. A one-day event could require up to 6-months of effort to see through the process.

Traditional Pillar 7 [tP7]:
Direct Marketing

Direct Marketing is a low cost method of reaching a particular target audience, relative to most other Traditional Pillars. It is analogous to Email Marketing, which is a subset of CRM (P5) and in general, utilizes a non-media, database driven approach towards targeting potential customers.

Includes:
Direct Response (TV and Radio); Informercials Direct Mail; Catalogs; Promotional Items.

Direct Mail is the most popular form of Direct Marketing. In this era of email and tech overload, people actually tend to read their mail with a greater attention span than their inbox. This provides local, national and even international businesses with the opportunity to elicit a response from a captive audience. When someone sends you a glossy catalog or a Fedex package, you will most likely open and look at it.

Direct Mail offers the ability to utilize list data or a company's own CRM database to segment audiences via geography, demographics and previous behavior (i.e. if they purchased particular products, visited certain places, etc.), and personalize messaging and offers based on what generally appeals to those audiences. At Blueliner, we have one vendor, for promotional items that we give away at trade shows, that mails us new sample items each month with our logos emblazoned and sure enough, guess who we keep going back to when it's time to order more swag? You got it!

Direct Marketing includes telemarketing and door-to-door sales, which overlaps with Sales (tP5). Other marketing tactics also have elements of Direct Marketing mixed with other Pillars, such as Direct Response TV (DRTV) and Radio which are technically forms of paid Advertising (tP3). Setting up a food truck or lemonade stand is a blend between Direct and Event Marketing.

The Marketing Dojo
Where Samurais Hone Their Craft

The 7 Modes

The 7 Modes (or Stages) of Marketing or Integrated Marketing represent the 2nd Dimension of the 7 Pillars System. The Modes apply to almost any consulting process or project, and certainly to all of Marketing, both digital and traditional. The Stages can still be referenced when it serves the purpose of a linear project progression, which is possible in very structured operations. The term "Modes" makes more sense as the official designation because "Stages" can (and often do) overlap, take place out of sequential order and be fairly continuous throughout projects.

The Modes are vital in the overall marketing process as each Mode is relevant to every Pillar. The Modes exist outside the Pillars and then intersect them, creating a 2-Dimensional grid called the 49er Matrix. The iconic 49er Matrix is one of the most visually intuitive and strategically effective tools that the 7 Pillars framework offers.

Before moving through the Modes, it is important to assess whether any of the Stages are already set in stone for various political reasons or management preferences. For example, there may be a Team (M4) and Budget (M2) already locked which answers some key questions and gives more focus for other areas of the project such as Strategy (M3).

Some key points to consider in relation to Modes:

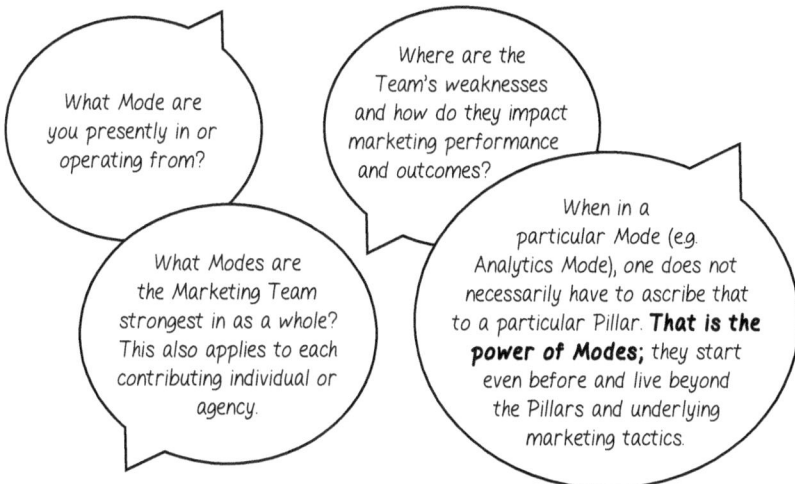

What Mode are you presently in or operating from?

Where are the Team's weaknesses and how do they impact marketing performance and outcomes?

What Modes are the Marketing Team strongest in as a whole? This also applies to each contributing individual or agency.

When in a particular Mode (e.g. Analytics Mode), one does not necessarily have to ascribe that to a particular Pillar. **That is the power of Modes;** they start even before and live beyond the Pillars and underlying marketing tactics.

Mode 1: Brainstorming

Synonyms:

Discovery;
Ideation;
Research Phase;
Free-flowing
ideas;
Q&A;
Scoping.

The Brainstorming Mode involves gathering and generating all types of ideas and information about whatever the vision at hand is, and how this can be attained. This covers research and data gathering from various sources, such as news and industry relevant websites.

It is a very important mindset to access at the beginning stages of any project. However, it doesn't end there. Brainstorming continues throughout the project as you continue to learn new things and refine your ideas. Anything goes in this Mode! Go vs. No-Go decisions should not be made in this Mode.

Ideation can be done collaboratively in real-time through 'brainstorming sessions', which can follow all types of formats or asynchronously, through email chains. It can also be done solo. Opinions tend to run high in this Mode, especially when applied to Pillars 1 (Content) and 2 (Design), which can be very subjective. This Mode is fun for most people but can drive certain types crazy, including those who want to organize and settle everything.

Succeeding in each Pillar's domain relies heavily on having good ideas – being creative, thoughtful and where possible, unique – instead of taking a cookie cutter approach to marketing. This naturally comes from having effective brainstormers on your team.

All of the world's best companies and ideas have been born from Mode 1. This is where the inspirational magic happens. However, be warned that moving too quickly to Budgeting and Strategy without allocating sufficient project team energy to Mode 1, can be a recipe for stale, uninspiring marketing.

Brainstorming tips:

1) Set aside individual and group time to brainstorm. Try to avoid Groupthink, during which
critical evaluation is stifled.

2) Take a different perspective. Put yourself in the shoes
of a competitor, child, manager, coach etc. and consider
how they might approach this issue.

3) Instead of writing out your ideas, draw or sketch them.

4) Create an 'idea map' that connects your thoughts.
Use mind mapping software like MindManager Pro by
Mindjet to do so.

5) Consider how you would approach the problem in a
different time period (e.g. 5 years ago, 5 years in the
future etc.)

It is important to note...

Brainstorming (M1) is generally an unstructured Mode
while other modes such as Analytics (M7), are typically
more Structured Modes.

1) Structured =
Ordered = Pre-Planned,
Repeatable Processes

2) Unstructured
= Agile = Fluid, Organic
and Responsive Ap-
proach = Less Linear

Neither are necessarily "correct" or better. Some circum-
stances and teams benefit from being more structured;
whereas certain campaigns and products are better
marketed in an unstructured format. Some people thrive
in structured environments, while others do better with
more flexibility. Later, we will also explore which Marketing
Personality Types (MPTs) and Angles are most effective in
particular Modes (e.g. Number Cruncher Types are ideal
for Budgeting Mode).

Mode 2: ROI

Synonyms:

Goal Setting;
Budgeting;
ROI Planing;
Return on
Investment;
KPIs;
Goals.

Mode 2 is where we develop and lock-in our forward-looking goals and associated budgets. It is closely related to the Financial Angle (see Chapter on Dimension 4, Angles, for details), although it is not at all a purely financial function. Goal-setting can and should be an inspiring and creative process.

There are so many variables that impact ROI, from evolving competition to seemingly endless marketing channels, that it can be daunting to develop and commit to tangible goals. The first step is to determine what your Key Performance Indicators (KPIs) are and if the organization has a history on which to evaluate past successes and challenges. This auditing process partially falls under Mode 7 (Analytics), which is more backward looking.

Based on the historical performance and present day mindset of key stakeholders (i.e. decision makers in the organization), Mode 2 requires a specific commitment to a budget that will be attributed towards the potential attainment of corresponding goals. Stakeholders and management have to collaborate on answering questions for specific upcoming periods (i.e. quarter, year, 3-year plan) such as:

How much money do we want to make? ie. Sales targets

What is our target Customer Acquisition Cost (by channel)?

What website traffic growth is projected?

How do we plan to allocate budgets across different marketing channels?

Those who spend time perfecting this Mode gain deep insights and accurate predictive ability into key assumptions that are integral for different marketing tactics (i.e. PPC conversion rates, Social Media impact).

This is one of many templates that have been developed under the 7 Pillars methodology, which are available in Excel and PDF format for download @ www.7pillarsdigital.com/roi or /m2.

Budget Allocation, Traffic Estimates, & Profitability Metrics:

	Jan 2016	Feb 2016	Mar 2016	Total (3 Months)
Media Fees (3rd Party)				
Agency Fees				
In-House Team Cost				
Web Traffic Targets				
Leads				
Customer/ Orders				
Revenues				

Mode 3: Strategy

Synonyms:

Planning;
Strategic
Planing;
Game Plan;
Approach.

This Mode comes into play when a project is underway. Here, ideas are more well-formed and organized plus areas such as budget and goals are nearly finalized. Now it's time for more focused research and planning of tactics for the campaign. Some tough decisions need to be made here, as many of the "nice to have" features and ideas are put on the chopping block due to budgetary constraints and/or strategic decisions to focus on more fruitful areas.

Strategy entails the creation and articulation of a marketing plan (utilizing 1 or more Pillars), based on all of the information provided and discovered through the other Modes. It requires high-level critical thinking and communication skills to convey the approach effectively to everyone involved in the project.

"we can't afford to wait"

Like Brainstorming (M1), Strategy is often skipped or shortchanged, typically out of impatience (e.g. "we can't afford to wait"), arrogance (e.g. "we don't need to plan") and/or lack of understanding (e.g. thinking strategy is merely selecting which marketing tactics to employ). The product of such thinking is what I call "Erratic Marketing", which is essentially hit or miss, and largely unproductive.

"we don't need to plan"

Strategy could be considered the first step in Execution (M6) but I regard it more as one of the final steps in Planning. It is imperative to have a sense for how specific tactical strategies (e.g. SEO Strategy) might impact the overall marketing strategy. Domain knowledge is of vital importance here, as strategies that work in one industry do not necessarily always carry across well to others. Good strategy requires a feel for which market segments are most promising and what existing resources may be effectively leveraged to target those segments.

The following table is just one of several
SEO Strategy templates that are used in 7 Pillars.
Find other @ **www.7pillarsdigital.com/m3**

	Sample Company Joe's Shoe Shack	Why is this important?	Strategy
Keyword List	online shoes, sneakers, custom leather shoes, dress shoes, orthotics	Website placement in Search Engines depends on how relevant your web-page content is to the keywords that users search.	Utilize the 7 Pillars Keyword Tiers System to prioritize the top 100 target keywords. Mix in high-volume phrases with long-tail, specific search terms (i.e. "brown italian leather men's shoes).
Link-Building	www.fashion-week.com/shoes, www.zappos.com/custom-shoes-partners	Off-page SEO plays a major role in how Search Engines determine the relevance of your website. More quality links = more "votes" of confidence to Search Engines.	Seek out fashionista bloggers and fashion writers who are active on Social Media, and seek product reviews with images and links back to website.
Blogging	How Our Shoes Are Made (Behind the Scenes); Protecting the Environment	Well-written blogs engage users and provide another opportunity to index quality content in Search Engines.	Use imagery, video and words to inspire the target audience and let them see into the company's ethos. Personal connection, not cold corporate.
KPI's & Analytics	Increase Organic Search Traffic by 200%; Attain at Least 25 1st Page Google Ranking (Within 6 Months)	Tracking the ebb and flow of organic search traffic and keyword ranking informs strategic changes that may be required.	Utilize dashboards and reporting from SEO tools like MOZ or Brightedge to update Keywords Tiers quarterly, and generate new content ideas.

Mode 4: **People**

Synonyms:

Teams;
Team Building;
Recruiting;
Human
Resources;
Casting;
Resourcing;
Scouting;
Performance
Management.

Mode 4 involves HR issues and decisions related to roles within marketing projects and specifically within each Pillar. Mode 4 represents the recruiting, team building, analysis, assignment, incentivizing, management and evaluation of the people involved in the project. From these areas, many questions abound. Who can execute the Strategy? What's the right mix of people by skill level, location, etc.? How do people and team dynamics impact timelines and ROI?

The whole 7 Pillars model relies entirely on People. In fact, each Pillar, each Block and each marketing tactic are similar to cells of a body, a holistic entity or person. The 49er Matrix is an analogy of people working together cohesively, each with a critical role to play in the big picture. This critical Mode should always be "On" in some sense. It is very typical to have the "wrong" person doing something that is not the best fit for them or the campaign and to have an uninspiring incentive structure.

Credentials are naturally imperative. It is necessary to have people with a solid level of skill and/or experience across the relevant Pillars. Let's say we're working on building out a Content Marketing team (i.e. a cross section of Pillar 1 and Mode 4, labeled Block 1.4 in the 49er Matrix). Block 1.4 is about the people that create content for a website, marketing campaign and overall digital strategy. Hence, we want skillful "Content Creators" and copywriters that are effective storytellers, preferably with experience in our industry.

Chemistry is equally important. If key stakeholders really want to shape the story but they don't vibe well with the Content Creators, the correct and best story won't be told.

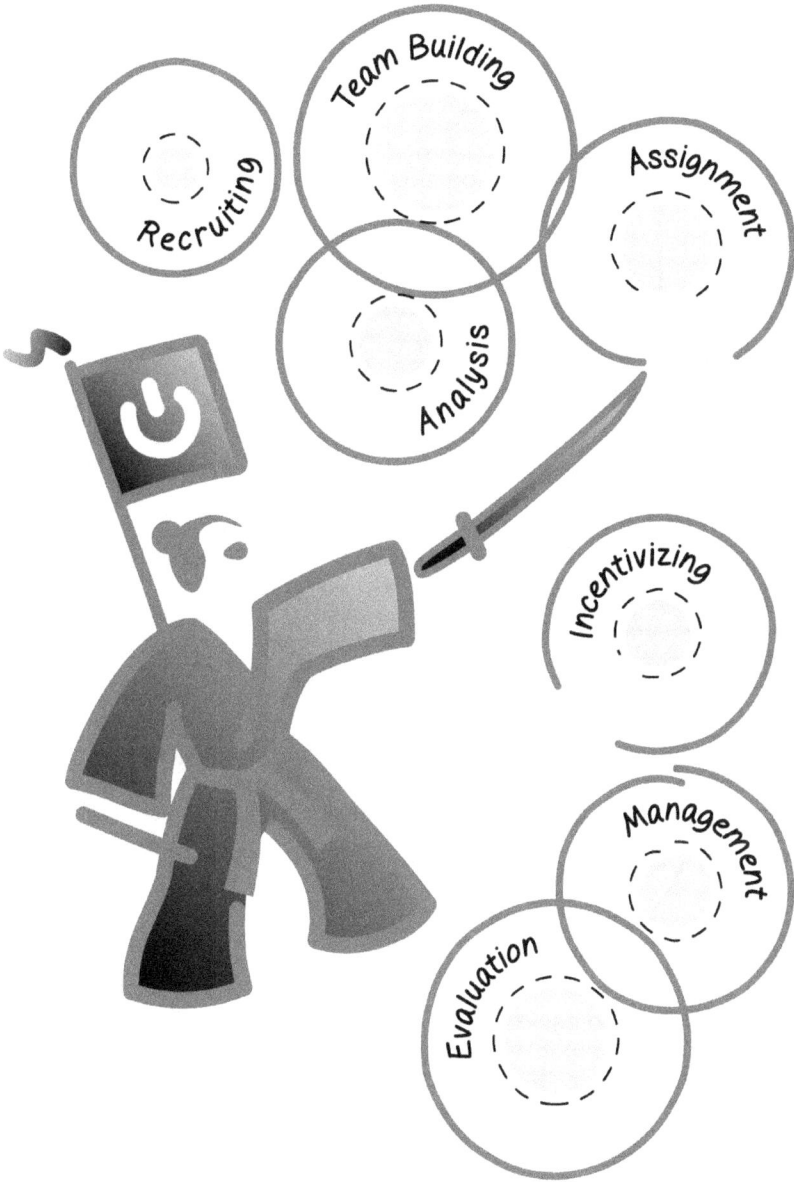

Effective M4 Management
Enables Successful Teams

Recruiting

Team Building

Assignment

Analysis

Incentivizing

Management

Evaluation

Mode 5: Tools

Synonyms:

Tech;
Systems.

Mode 5 refers to the tools and technology that may be utilized to organize, manage and analyze various types of marketing and web development (i.e. Salesforce.com for CRM, Mailchimp for Email, WordPress for website Content Management and Google Adwords for Online Advertising). Picking the right tools, based on project budgets (Mode 2) and the people involved (Mode 4), can save a team hundreds of hours of "wasted," manual effort, and play a huge role in a campaign's success.

Many questions abound:

What tools do the current team prefer or are they most comfortable working with?

Who is in charge of evaluating the effectiveness of the current portfolio of tools, as well as potentially new ones?

Is there a budget for training staff on new systems, which could increase efficiency and campaign insights?

What level of automation are we comfortable with, versus manual effort and communications with clients?

In this day and age of productivity apps, mobile accessibility and cloud SaaS programs, marketers are bombarded with "the next best thing" promises all day long. This can cause a bit of "App Fatigue," and have the reverse effect; it can make a team less efficient, because they are always searching for the "perfect" tools to solve all of their business problems instead of making due with the ones already being used within the organization. I recommend that you don't chase this fantasy. Keep it simple, and do your diligence, test drive before subscribing to systems, ensure that key people become super users, and stay committed to a compact set of tools that streamline your process.

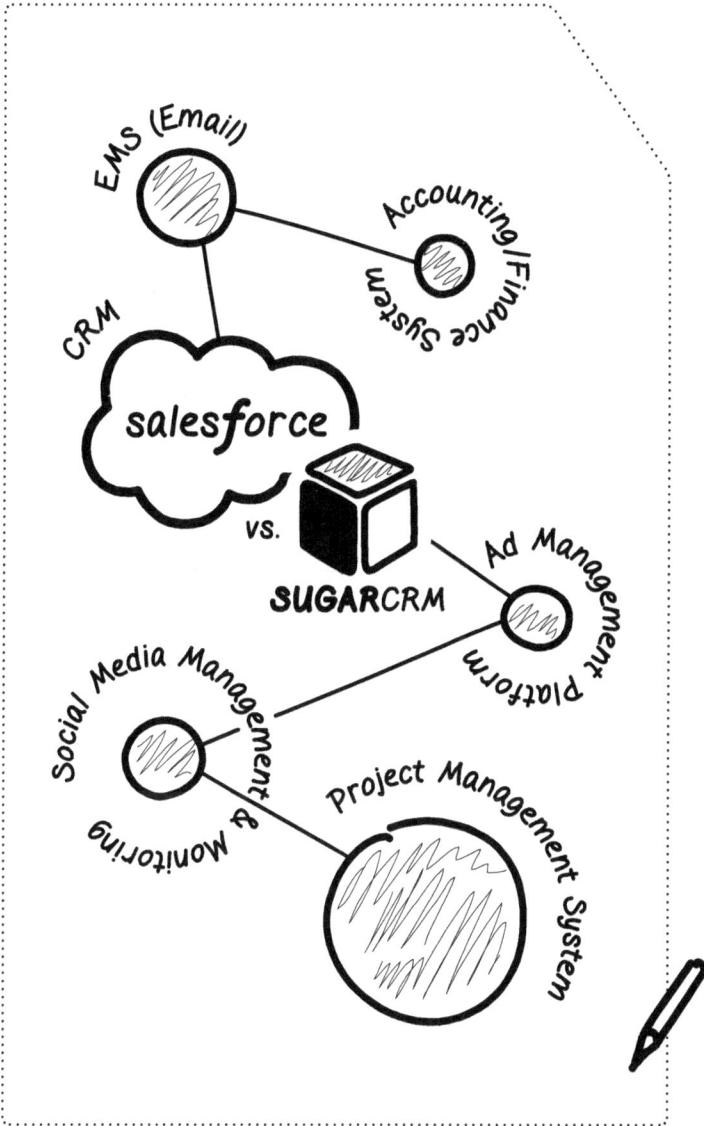

Mode 6: **Execution**

Execution refers to the actual doing of the tactical work. With people, budgets, tools and strategies in place, Mode 6 is where the rubber meets the road. If Digital Marketing was a sports league, this would be actual game day.

All other Modes refer to some type of pre-game preparation (e.g. practice, draft) or post-game analysis (e.g. watching game film, grading performances). Execution features a distinction between management (people managing the work) and actual implementation (people doing the work). In startups, smaller companies and agencies, this line is often blurred, as Project Managers also do some of the hands-on work, in parallel as they manage projects. I personally believe in active managers, as opposed to hands-off delegators. If you get too far away from the hands-on work, it's a fast way to become outdated and obsolete.

Here you can observe the interconnectedness of the Modes. What are the chances of effective Execution, if other Modes (or Stages) were not given proper fuel. For example, envision Brainstorming had been skipped, Budget shortchanged, Strategy left vague, People half-committed and Tools still undecided? Even a super strong Execution team will run into problems if this were the situation and it happens all the time! It costs money and takes a certain approach to properly fuel and juggle all of the Modes.

The opposite is also true; getting other Stages setup well, and then executing poorly can spoil the best laid plans. The good news is that everything, especially Execution issues, is correctable and teachable, if the key stakeholders remain objective and are committed to success.

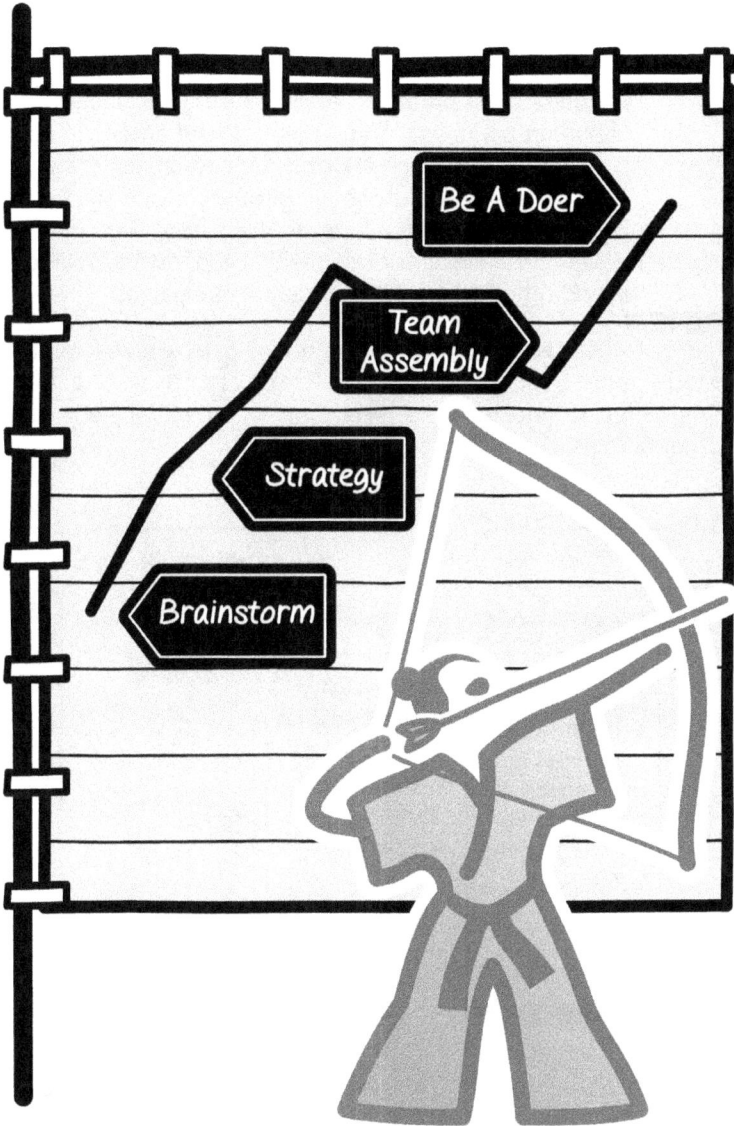

Don't just sit on a plan
execute it!

Be A Doer

Team Assembly

Strategy

Brainstorm

Mode 7: **Analytics**

Synonyms:

Optimization;
Analysis;
Auditing;
Business
Intelligence.

The final Mode, which can take place to some degree throughout the whole marketing process, refers to campaign analysis and recommendation generation for optimization purposes. Analytics can be likened to the human brain, as it is the memory and analytical mind within us. Analytics involve taking an objective look at all of the data and signals throughout the marketing process and across whatever Pillars have been utilized. This Mode is critical to making judgments, revisions and other critical decisions about campaigns.

Google Analytics is one of the typical hubs for this Mode, as are Google Adwords, SEO Rankings software (e.g. Moz, BrightEdge, Conductor), Excel reporting, Domo and a plethora of other BI tools. Key Analytical tasks include:

Determining how success is going to be measured (what are our KPIs)? This conversation begins in Stage 2 (ROI Planning) but here is where teams actually start measuring marketing performance.

Set Campaign Review schedule at which time KPIs will be assessed and measured.

Determine Responsible Person and other Stakeholders for Audits, of your own or another team's work (e.g. let's say you're an agency coming in to replace another agency).

Each Mode, including Analytics, is a microcosm of the whole marketing process, and hence itself pertains to all of the Modes. For example, Analytics needs to be brainstormed, strategized for, budgeted sufficiently, executed well and have its own performance analyzed. This Mode also needs to have proficient People involved and proper Tools in place. In this way, Analytics (M7) most resembles the Pillars, in that it can be treated as its own stand-alone category of marketing.

Audit Exercise
(i.e. Analysis of Takeover Campaign):

The previous agency was abruptly fired and your team is now on board to take over a running campaign. What do you need to know?

1) *What was the previous agency's reporting format and timing? Obtain as many historical reports as possible, to study what the baseline efforts and results have been.*

2) *Get Google Analytics access right away, and run trend reports on historical traffic over the past year.*

3) *Was there a set of benchmarks that were in place before? Either way, work with the client to create a new one now, that everyone can buy into.*

4) *What creative, copy and ads have performed better than expected?*

5) *What are the PPC and CPM results currently?*

6) *How many skilled marketers do we need on this account, and from which disciplines?*

7) *Review CRM and EMS (Email Marketing) reports, to evaluate how effectively the base is engaged.*

The 49er Matrix
at play

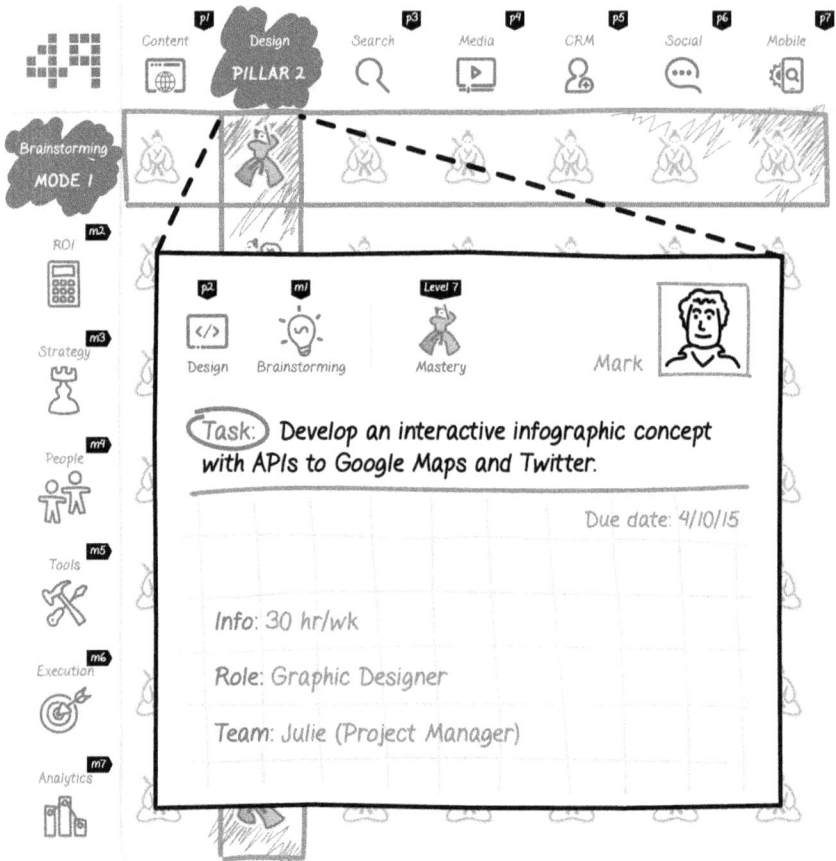

| | Content | Design PILLAR 2 | Search | Media | CRM | Social | Mobile |
| | p1 | Design | p3 | p4 | p5 | p6 | p7 |

Brainstorming MODE 1

ROI m2
Strategy m3
People m4
Tools m5
Execution m6
Analytics m7

p2 Design | **m1** Brainstorming | **Level 7** Mastery | Mark

Task: Develop an interactive infographic concept with APIs to Google Maps and Twitter.

Due date: 4/10/15

Info: 30 hr/wk

Role: Graphic Designer

Team: Julie (Project Manager)

For blank 49er Matrix templates,
visit www.7pillarsdigital.com/matrix

The 49er Matrix can be thought of as a 7-Dimensional Chess Board, upon which we play out the strategic game of Marketing. It is a multi-purpose visualization tool that provides a map of the Digital Marketing universe. The first two dimensions (7 Pillars x 7 Modes) generate 49 blocks or marketing elements, which marketers and executives should account for.

The 49er Matrix provides an effective structure for the organization of marketing knowledge. It has many practical uses, particularly as a template for Marketing Audits and Plans for individuals, companies, agencies, campaigns, projects, websites and products. Here is a partial list of **49er Matrix applications** that assist marketers with assessment and planning efforts:

The 49er Matrix App can help you...

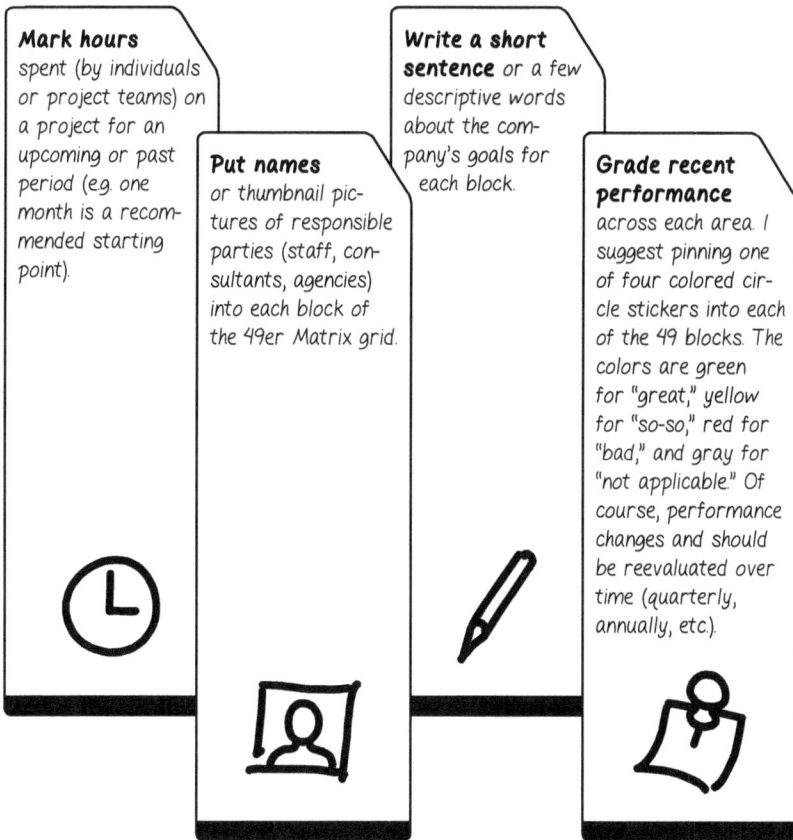

Mark hours spent (by individuals or project teams) on a project for an upcoming or past period (e.g. one month is a recommended starting point).

Put names or thumbnail pictures of responsible parties (staff, consultants, agencies) into each block of the 49er Matrix grid.

Write a short sentence or a few descriptive words about the company's goals for each block.

Grade recent performance across each area. I suggest pinning one of four colored circle stickers into each of the 49 blocks. The colors are green for "great," yellow for "so-so," red for "bad," and gray for "not applicable." Of course, performance changes and should be reevaluated over time (quarterly, annually, etc.).

A career path

The 7 Angles (or Tracks)

Envision a large Pyramid laying on top of the 49er Matrix grid, the pinnacles of which represents the culmination of digital marketing knowledge. The Angles represent the sides or ways up the Pyramids. Individuals choose to ascend the Pyramid (developing their skills) up one of the main sides or one of the corners.

There are three Flat Angles which correspond to the four main sides of the Pyramid; and four Sharp Angles, which correspond to the four corners of the Pyramid (see diagram below). The Flats have more specificity to marketing, broader career opportunities, generally more tasks and are more conductive to a broader group of people. Meanwhile, the Sharps are critical components with more specialized skill sets that help to shape and organize the Pillars, and consequently, the Universe of Marketing.

Angles Pyramid Aerial View (Angles x Levels)

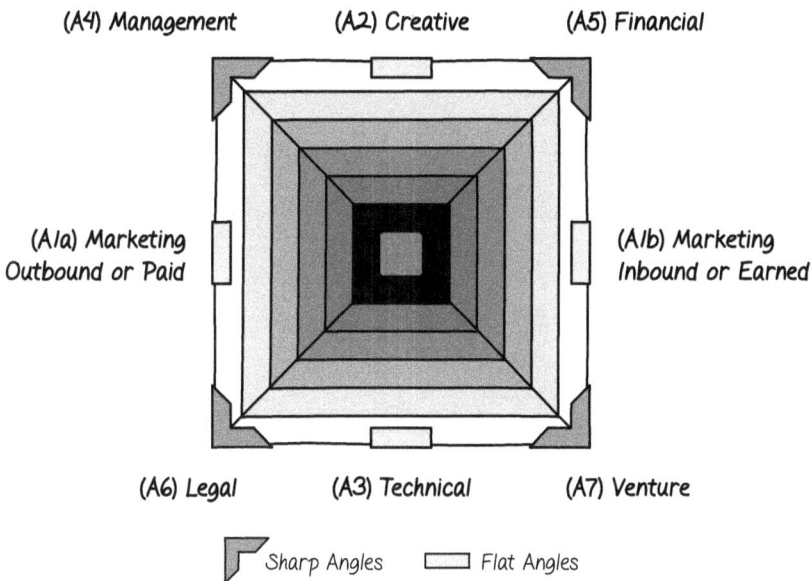

(A4) Management   (A2) Creative   (A5) Financial

(A1a) Marketing
Outbound or Paid

(A1b) Marketing
Inbound or Earned

(A6) Legal   (A3) Technical   (A7) Venture

Sharp Angles   Flat Angles

It generally makes sense to focus 2-3 Angles; otherwise, one can tend to get stuck at certain points in their career, forcing the person to reinvent him or herself.

D1 D2 **D3** D4 D5 D6 D7

Angle 1 [A1]: ☐ Flat ☐

Marketing

Includes:

Media buyers;
Paid Search
managers;
Strategic
thinkers;
Researchers;
Copywriters;
Social Media
Specialists.

Angle 1 is the most popular and diverse within the 7 Pillars ecosystem, naturally because this is a marketing system after all! People who take this primary track generally aren't programmers or designers. Their value comes through having more of a promotional sense of what needs to be done to build brands and generate leads. They are pure marketers (i.e. strategic thinkers, researchers, media buyers, copywriters and general doers of non-technical marketing tasks). Their energy is one of communicating, presenting and selling ideas. Their main purpose is lead generation and raising brand awareness, through either paid or earned media which are split within this Flat Angle into two diametrically opposed approaches.

A1a) Paid Media and Outbound Marketing. Tactics like Pay Per Click Advertising are included, because in this channel, we must pay for placement.

A1b) Earned Media and Inbound Marketing. Tactics like SEO are included, because here, we gain placement through creative, non-paid media efforts.

Quick Tips

1) Experiment with different tools and strategies, in order to find the right marketing mix.

2) Partner up with masters of different Angles, to benefit from collaboration.

3) Don't forget about traditional marketing strategies, which complement digital marketing.

4) Determine whether your natural strengths and tendencies lie more with Outbound (A1a) or Inbound (A1b) Marketing.

Features of the Marketing Angle

Most Common Pillars:

Content (P1), Search (P3), Media (P4), CRM (P5) and Social Media (P6).

Most Common Tasks:

Copywriting, Media Buying, Strategic Planning, Pitching new Business, Presentations, Analytics & Reporting, Marketing Research, Competitive Analysis, Email & Newsletter Communications, Social Media Marketing, SEO.

Most Conducive MPTs:*

Information Gatherer (MPT2), Hunter (MPT3), Brainstormer (MPT5), Doer (MPT6).

Favorite Modes:

Brainstorming (M1), Strategy (M3), People (M4), Execution (M6).

Complementary Angles:

Creative (A2), Venture (A7).

*MPTs are Marketing Personality Types, which are covered on Pages 113-121. There are 7 Types.

Angle 2 [A2]: Flat
Creative

Includes:

Graphic designers;
Web designers;
Sketch artists;
Animators;
Photographers;
Videographers;
Creative writers.

The Creative Angle (A2) is represented by the right brain artists amongst us. While creativity is certainly a quality that can permeate all Angles, this area is focused primarily on the audio-visual content that dominates our senses. Certain skills, like writing, bisect, falling under A2 for creative content like fiction and storytelling, and A1 (Marketing Angles) for ad and product description focused copy.

The Creative Angle manifests and is needed almost everywhere across Digital Marketing as it is the energy which most directly impacts Branding (tP2). As a career path, A2s can travel in a lot of directions once they start reaching the higher Levels of their trade. They are well-served to complement their skills with one or more of the other tracks as a path towards taking ownership of not only Branding but the overall business development process.

Quick Tips

1) Getting feedback from team members and stakeholders is key.

2) Consider learning some tactics from the Marketing Angles as well, to complement Creative skills.

3) Take some chances with design. Think outside the box, so that your concepts don't fall into the "cookie cutter" category.

4) Study and respect traditional design and Branding - the principles of which hold firm within digital creative as well.

5) Healthy chaos during the creative process is encouraged; but it's also important to stay organized.

6) If you're in a creative rut, take a mental break and clear your mind with a 15+ minute breathing meditation!

Features of the Creative Angle

Most Common Pillars:

Content (P1), UX (P2), Social (P6), Mobile (P7).

Most Common Tasks:

Graphical Design, Hi-Fi Wireframing via Photoshop or comparable tools, Web Design, App Design, Brand Design, Video Editing, Video Filming, Presentation Design, Product Design, Animation, Photography, Music Composition, Style Guide (Brand Guidelines) Creation.

Most Conducive MPTs:

Brainstormer (MPT5), Doer (MPT 6), Visionary (MPT7).

Favorite Modes:

Brainstorming (M1), Strategy (M3), Tools (M5), Execution (M6).

Complementary Angles:

Marketing (A1).

Angle 3 [A3]: Flat

Technical

Angle 3 includes programmers, technologists and the overall technical backbone of the Internet. This covers the Internet as well as advanced infrastructure required to support apps (i.e. the cloud and mobile technology). Non-technical marketers should remember and respect the fact that Digital Marketing is made possible by the capabilities of A3s, who built all of the software tools that they use.

What makes this Angle all the more powerful is the increasingly collaborative nature of Internet and Mobile tech. Movements like crowdsourcing and open source development are prime examples. This is a fantastic track to be part of because of the vast support resources available, which make building sophisticated software easier then ever. Increasingly, "techies" are being tapped for senior positions at companies, and are becoming more integrated, as opposed to isolated, from teammates in other divisions.

Quick Tips

Technical Angle Cheat Sheet

How "technical" am I, relative to my co-workers?

① ② ③ ④ ⑤ ⑥ ⑦

What are my go-to technical skills, that I can be depended on to deliver?

If I could easily learn one new technical skill, what would it be?

Who are my go-to techies if I need to get some challenging coding projects done?

Features of the Technical Angle

Most Common Pillars:

UX (P2), Mobile (P7).

Most Common Tasks:

Wireframing, Functional Specification Writing, Coding (Programming), App Development, Technical Research, QA (Quality Assurance) Testing, API Development & Integration, Tech Admin (i.e. Web Hosting Setup & Maintenance, Email Setup, Network Administration), SDK Creation & Learning, Technical Documentation.

Most Conducive MPTs:

Number Cruncher (MPT1), Information Gatherer (MPT2), Farmer (MPT4), Doer (MPT6).

Favorite Modes:

Discovery (M1), Tools (M5), Execution (M6), Analytics (M7).

Complementary Angles:

Financial (A5), Legal (A6).

Angle 4 [A4]: Sharp Management

Management (A4), the first of four Sharp Angles, keeps projects together and gives direction to them. It is essential, both as a skill and an overall function in any company, and it is something that needs to be developed throughout a person's career. It can also be a slippery slope, especially if not developed alongside some "hard" skills (i.e. those of the Flat Angles). Digital Marketing is an open field where many resources are accessible and interchangeable. My mentor, David Houle, author of The Shift Age™, discusses increasing disintermediation due to digital technology and infrastructure changes in society. For example, this occurs when Buyers and Sellers cut out the middle man (e.g. a stock broker) and "go direct." Career managers are subject to the same forces.

Management is prevalent and needed along all 7 Pillars and 49er Matrix blocks. Green and Brown belts tend to be Managers while Black and Blue belts generally act more at the executive level.

Quick Tips

1) Allot weekly time for individual 'check-in' and progress meetings with staff.

2) Observe, listen and learn your team's strengths and weaknesses.

3) Assign staff to positions and projects that they feel are the best fit for them.

4) Set achievable and realistic deadlines and benchmarks.

5) Don't break promises or push back your own deadlines - you run the risk of bottlenecking your staff's progress.

6) Everyone has limitations - know yours.

7) Recognize - celebrate - your team's achievements. Positive reinforcement goes a long way.

Features of the Management Angle

Most Common Pillars:

All

Most Common Tasks:

Project Management, Task List Creation, Report Generation, Leading Meetings, Presentation Development, Budgeting, Performance Reviews, HR (Recruiting), Strategic Planning.

Most Conducive MPTs:

Number Cruncher (MPT1), Farmer (MPT4).

Favorite Modes:

ROI (M2), Strategy (M3), People (M4), Analytics (M7).

Complementary Angles:

Technical (A3), Financial (A5), Legal (A6).

Angle 5 [A5]: Sharp Financial

Advice:

Every Project Manager, Account Manager and division leader ought to have a strong Financial repertoire, including the ability to put together budgets, ROI Plans and channel-based performance reports.

Every industry has a strong need for Financial folks. In Digital Marketing, they get to have even stronger powers because of the vast toolbox available to them. This Sharp Angle belongs to the Number Cruncher (MPT1), who spend time mostly in Budgeting (M2) and Analytics (M7) Modes. Beyond pure finance jobs (i.e. Accountants and Financial Analysts) the Financial skill set helps guide projects, and keeps them on track and on budget.

A5 is all the more important because of the rapid changes in technology and pricing of just about everything. Plus, the movement of global money, due to services like Paypal, is accelerating and scaling at breakneck pace. Gone are the years of the 5-year budget. Things are changing too fast for that and A5s are responsible for ensuring that the company's metrics and KPIs are keeping up.

Quick Tips

Use this spreadsheet to help develop a reasonable project budget:

Agency Fees	Jan 2016	Feb 2016	March 2016
P3 Search			
P4 Media			
P5 CRM			
P6 Social			
3rd Party Budgets			
P3 Search (Link Building)			
P4. Media (PPC, Retargeting)			
P5. CRM (Email EMS Fees)			
P6. Social (Boosts, Ads)			
Total Monthly Budget			

Features of the Financial Angle

Most Common Pillars:

All

Most Common Tasks:

Budgeting, ROI Marketing Plan Development, Analytics & Reporting, Board Presentations, Banking, Proposal Creation & Review, Negotiating Contracts.

Most Conducive MPTs:

Number Cruncher (MPT1), Information Gatherer (MPT2), Farmer (MPT4).

Favorite Modes:

ROI & Budgeting (M2), Tools (M5), Analytics (M7).

Complementary Angles:

Technical (A3), Management (A4), Legal (A6).

Angle 6 [A6]: Sharp

Legal

Advice:

Know when to call in a legal or compliance specialist, especially if you work in a regulated industry. And add extra weeks to your project timelines, to account for compliance issues and delays.

Yes, lawyers have a place in the 7 Pillars ecosystem, as defenders, interpreters and creators of the laws that govern media and the Internet. It is a vast space, which has confounded governments and legal systems that have been, and largely still are, ill-equipped to deal with such a powerful force of inter-connection and cross-border trade. Think back to Napster and other piracy issues, which are difficult to police and raise all types of ethical questions. How about the NSA, Facebook, Google vs. China and Internet privacy? This is another field of debate that A6 specialists moderate for organizations.

There are key industries that garner billions of marketing dollars – most notably Pharmaceuticals – which are highly regulated. People whose primary Angle is Legal comprise the compliance teams that govern and review marketing materials.

It is interesting to witness how the Legal field has evolved through the use of digital technology, such as digital signatures and template sharing (e.g. LegalZoom). It opens the door for some reckless self-lawyering and manipulation for those who either have malicious intent or don't have proper Legal support. Through experience, you will learn when you need to call in a lawyer, versus simply paying more attention to various paperwork and terms that you are agreeing to.

Lastly, most websites - especially SaaS - have a privacy policy and terms of agreement. That's all A6 territory.

The Legal Angle is the most overlooked angle but it is vastly important

Most Common Pillars:

All

Most Common Tasks:

Reviewing and Negotiating Contracts, Legal Advice, Compliance Reviews.

Most Conducive MPTs:

Information Gatherer (MPT2), Farmer (MPT4).

Favorite Modes:

Strategy (M3), Execution (M6), Analytics (M7).

Complementary Angles:

Tech (A3), Management (A4), Financial (A5).

Angle 7 [A7]: Sharp Venture

A7 is the realm of the entrepreneurs and venture capitalists seeking to create and control how the Internet runs. New ventures, from players who seek to influence and improve web tools, pop up daily within each Pillar.

Since the dawn of the Internet in 1993, entrepreneurs and investors alike have flocked to the web in order to claim their share of the virtual gold rush. Honing in on Mode 5 (Tools & Tech), you'll witness a plethora of success stories as well as failures in this digital arms race. The good news is that, like the Big Bang, the Internet, including the mobile web, is an ever-expanding universe that now touches almost 6 billion of the Earth's inhabitants. Therefore, there is a lot of room for more people to own and participate in their fair share of the ecosystem.

It is important to follow both startups and established companies in the realm, in order to keep up with the trends and best available tools for whatever your specialty is. It is easier than ever to become out of date; the proponents of A7 are making sure of that!

Exercise:

1) How much A7 do you have within you?

① ② ③ ④ ⑤ ⑥ ⑦

2) If you were given $1 million and tasked to start a new company in the tech field that aims to make a 10x ROI within 5 years or less, what type of company would you start?

3) List 1-2 cool, game-changing innovations (either new companies or new products from existing companies) across your favorite Pillars, or even all 7 of them.

Features of the Venture Angle

Most Common Pillars:

All

Most Common Tasks:

Startup Investing, Startup Business Plan Writing, Ideation, Brand Strategy Development, Marketing Plan Creation, Financial Plan Creation, Pitching Investors, Recruiting Talent (HR), Software Development.

Most Conducive MPTs:

Number Cruncher (MPT1), Information Gatherer (MPT2), Hunter (MPT3), Doer (MPT6), Visionary (MPT7).

Favorite Modes:

Ideation (M1), Strategy (M3), Tools (M5).

Complementary Angles:

Marketing (A1), Creative (A2), Technical (A3).

Assessing
our own level

The 7 Levels [of Skill & Difficulty]

Your career - in business and marketing - is analogous to the journey that aspiring Samurai warriors embark upon as they seek personal truth and mastery of their craft. True progress is not easy. It is elusive, which represent the Levels are symbolized by Pyramids (or Temples), which represent the uphill battle required to raise oneself up. Only the most skillful and perseverant digital martial artist ascends to the top and achieves the vaunted Blue Samurai status.

Just like in the karate dojo, marketing practitioners progress in ability through the years, hopefully under the direction of one or more strong teachers, managers, mentors or role models. Everything moves faster in the Digital Age, including the skill levels of ambitious and hard-working Samurais. 7 Pillars breaks everything down into 7 Levels of skill (of the individual) and corresponding difficulty (of the task). For example, a Level 2 SEO marketer should be able to manage Level 1 and Level 2 SEO tasks without a problem. However, Level 3 tasks might present some challenges for this individual.

Levels apply to each Pillar, Mode and all Dimensions in fact, calling for the evaluation of team and campaigns, as well as individuals. This can be done quite effectively by using the 49er Matrix app or template.

It is very difficult to truly assess skill level. Standardized testing, degrees and certifications don't tell the whole story. Management reviews can undersell themselves. As a result, managers and marketing teams are often understaffed and ill-prepared for certain levels of work, and the results generally show it.

That said, it is vital to get a sense for everyone's level, and to develop a common language that allows managers to setup project teams to match the requisite difficulty level of the projects at hand.

You should know your true level, for a variety of reasons. Most importantly, it empowers you to be practical about what type of work your are best suited to execute well and allows you to focus on what skills you need to develop.

Every Dimension in the 7 Pillars model is a further segmentation of the previous one. At this stage, Levels as the 4th Dimension, provides added perspective to the 3rd Dimension - Angles. While Angles give information on *how* someone is coming up (i.e. Technical vs. Creative Angle), Levels tell us *how far* they have climbed. A key benefit to higher ranking Samurais is the ability to crossover from one Angle to another. For example, a Level 4 UX Technician can more easily learn and become a UX Manager than one at Level 3.

Two key visuals are utilized to depict Levels:

1) the 7 Samurais of Eastern (Japanese) martial arts correspond to the 7 Levels and

2) the Pyramids reflect the journey to the top of the trade.

Pyramids are perfectly analogous because they convey how there are multiple Angles to the top and also that there is less room at each successive level, due to the Law of Inertia. Not everyone really wants to go to the top, because it requires a great deal of effort and sacrifice to do so! That is alright - one just has to be honest with themselves as far as what they really want to achieve in this domain.

The rest of this Chapter describes what types of Tasks and Skills are typically seen at the respective 7 Levels.

7 Samurais = 7 Levels

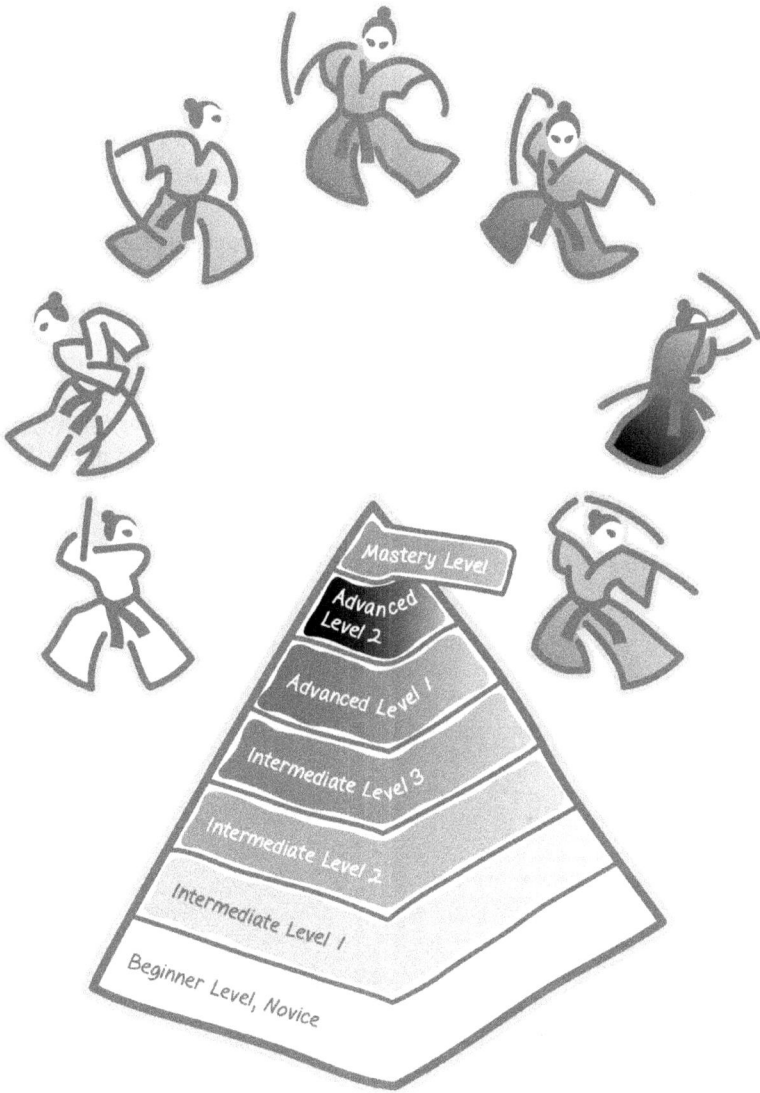

Mastery Level

Advanced Level 2

Advanced Level 1

Intermediate Level 3

Intermediate Level 2

Intermediate Level 1

Beginner Level, Novice

Level I: White Belt

Beginner Level, Novice

In general, a newcomer enters the dojo (i.e. the marketing realm) with some core skills (i.e. writing, quantitative, research). However, in marketing terms, he or she is still a pure beginner. The teacher or Sensei's job, assuming the novice is not being purely self-taught, is to assess these skills and then determine what types of basic building blocks they need to learn in order to complement their transferrable skills. In a marketing department or agency, white belts are typically interns or entry-level trainees, titled Analysts, but not always.

White belts are very raw in this field, and although they may be smart people (PhDs, MDs, and even CEOs), their digital IQ, for whatever reason, has not yet been developed. On the following page is a quick chart of what kinds of task white belts generally perform within each Pillar, most of which involve active learning and research.

Exercise:

Imagine that you are a White Belt, or think about a White Belt level person in your organization. What are some reasonable goals? Using the 49er matrix, map out how the white belt will accomplish these goals. Considering a novice's strengths and weaknesses within each Pillar and Mode, formulate a strategy for how to build-up several particular skills that are important for growth.

A White Belt Should be Able to...

P1. Content

Research and analyze leading publishers and bloggers in respective industry.

P2. UX

Learn the basics of graphical and web design packages, like Photoshop, Illustrator or Wordpress.

P3. Search

Learn the basics of keyword research tools, like Google Adwords Keyword Research Tool.

P4. Media

Create a Google Adwords account and study Cost Per Click pricing for keywords relevant to his or her field.

P5. CRM

Review basic CRM and Email platforms, (i.e. Salesforce and Mailchimp) and grasp the concept of segmentation.

P6. Social

Identify relevant groups or build target lists of potential connections on one or more social networks.

P7. Mobile

Download/use several leading smartphone apps.

Level 2: Yellow Belt

Yellow Belts are on the cusp between Beginner and Intermediate levels of knowledge. They've learned something and have minimal experience of at least 3-6 months. A fast learner without a long track record but who has a knack for Digital Marketing could make the jump to Yellow Belt very quickly. In smaller companies, this tends to happen as junior level people start taking on tasks or roles that stretch their capabilities. This could be potentially beneficial to their growth but also dangerous - in terms of project quality - if they don't have proper supervision or feedback.

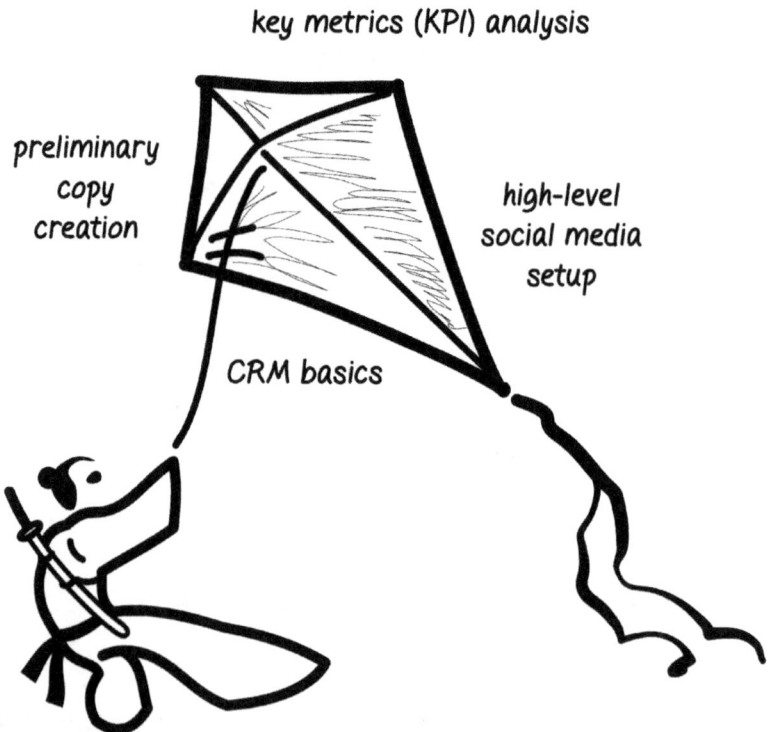

key metrics (KPI) analysis

preliminary copy creation

high-level social media setup

CRM basics

Yellow Belts can comfortably...

P1. Content

Identify stock images and write basic copy for websites.

P2. UX

Utilize Analytics tools like Google Analytics to assess Calls To Action (CTAs) and landing pages for success factors.

P3. Search

Put together keyword lists and research competitors.

P4. Media

Basic comprehension of CPM (Cost per Thousand Impressions) media rate cards and common display banner ad sizes.

P5. CRM

Setup and/or enter data into CRM and Email platforms, with the ability to search for key information and generate reports.

P6. Social

Setup basic business profiles, design and copy wise, on more than one social network.

P7. Mobile

Analyze differences in key metrics (i.e. Time on Site, % of Traffic) between mobile, tablet and desktop users of websites.

Level 3: Orange Belt

Intermediate Level 2

Orange Belts are marketers with solid experience, typically having been in "the game" for at least two years. As individuals progress in their marketing journey, what they know goes beyond theoretical and has the taste of practical experience and real knowledge. This is the most crowded Level in the industry, along with Green Belt.

Orange Belts, while still in a critical phase of their learning curve, are capable of executing a good deal of the hands-on marketing tasks.

They key for L3s is to stay at it, and focus on choosing one or two Pillars and Modes to dive even deeper in. With a good base in place, now is the time to start making moves towards some type of expertise.

Quick Tips

1) Don't juggle too many tasks at the same time - it will dilute your efforts.

2) Develop a 2-year career vision and plan to get there.

3) If you get stuck in the minutia of a particular assignment, don't get lost in it; shift gears to something else, or take a break, and come back fresh.

4) Gain mastery over your time, by paying close attention to how long things take for you to get done (Core Principle 1).

5) Share your knowledge with team members of all levels - lower, higher and peers.

6) Keep your momentum rolling - learn new skills across the Pillars, Modes and Angles as often as possible.

Orange Belts can...

P1. Content

Write blogs and website copy; Generate taglines and titles for sections of copy; Produce audio, photo and video content.

P2. UX

Put together a basic sitemap, design static web page comps and write standard use cases.

P3. Search

Refine keyword lists, map them to pages in the sitemap and write metadata that aligns with target keywords.

P4. Media

Setup and manage small PPC accounts, including writing ad copy, bidding on keywords and basic reporting.

P5. CRM

Setup and manage basic Email Marketing campaigns; Generate Web Analytics reports for different user segments.

P6. Social

Operate social profiles, including original content posts, hash tagging, promotion (boosting), engagement and reporting.

P7. Mobile

Research and advise on location-based strategies.

Level 4: Green Belt

Intermediate Level 3

Green Belts are on the verge of being true domain experts, and relative to some, may already be considered as experts. They have enough experience (generally 3-4 years) to manage campaigns independently. At the agency level, Green Belts typically project manage (PM) smaller projects and even do some training for clients or entry level staff (White, Yellow and Orange Belts). There are many freelancers in the market at this level, who have developed confidence through their path and realize that they have a lot to offer, and can charge a good hourly rate for their services.

Being right in the middle of the 7 Levels, Green Belts are generally the hardest workers. They are no longer beginners yet are not yet at the top of the mountain or generally calling shots. Therefore, they are leaned on heavily to be hands-on.

Anyone who has made it to this level has proven to me that they are serious about this career path, and have the will to climb the mountain.

Guiding Advice

Create a growth strategy and implementation plan by:

1) Writing down your 6 month - 2 year vision for a current project (i.e. what are your target KPIs?)

2) Brainstorming on how to bring together a cohesive team (i.e. who will work well together and add value?)

3) Involving the client/stakeholders in the project goals early on.

4) Being resourceful and thorough in analyzing which Tech Tools to utilize on the project.

5) Taking ownership of the downfalls and successes of the project.

A Green Belt can confidently...

P1. Content

Create and manage editorial calendars; Direct commercials and photo shoots.

P2. UX

Design multi page-state wireframes for desktop and mobile; low fidelity (i.e. sketches) and high fidelity (graphics).

P3. Search

Create SEO Plans; Execute Schema microformats; Perform ongoing Link Building; produce detailed SEO Reports.

P4. Media

Setup mid-sized, complex PPC accounts, with use of 3rd party ad platforms; Create media plans that mix in CPA and CPM.

P5. CRM

Customize CRM software to specific industry/company needs; Integrate modules and APIs; implement automation tools.

P6. Social

Create Social Media Plans; Integrate Social within other channels; Report on ROI, attribution and influence of Social tactics.

P7. Mobile

Scope out mobile sites & apps; App store promotion.

Level 5: Brown Belt

Advanced Level I

An individual can become a Brown belt in anywhere from 2-5 years, depending on the level of real experience they get on a particular track. Brown belts must have authored at least two tangible 'successes' that can be clearly demonstrated and potentially replicated by them. At this Level, strategy, communications and integration across Pillars take on more importance, presenting opportunities to flourish for these skilled Samurais.

Brown belts generally have strong knowledge across at least 3 Pillars. They are skilled technicians that are typically hands-on project leads and have also developed some level of teaching, delegation and management skills.

Give me a Brown belt, and I'll give you a future Marketing Director or Head of Digital Strategy in two years or less.

Exercise:

Identify and classify the 3 Pillars that you are currently most knowledgeable in. What have you learned to date and what do you need to learn in each of these 3 Pillars in order to rise to the next Level? What steps do you need to take to build your skill sets in each Pillar? Determine someone that you consider at a higher Level (Black or Blue) and interview them, to identify your strengths and weaknesses across the 3 chosen Pillars.

A Brown Belt should be able to...

P1. Content

Be a skilled content strategist and producers, including blog and book authorship, as well as complex video/commercial production.

P2. UX

Run and optimize complex multi-variate tests; Oversee major Web Development projects; Oversee or execute advanced software programming.

P3. Search

Generate and take responsibility for SEO results in competitive industries; Run complex SEO audits; develop advanced SEO strategies.

P4. Media

Manage sophisticated media campaigns, including retargeting, ROI and attribution amidst PPC, CPA and CPM.

P5. CRM

Run multi-location CRM Strategy, as well as marketing automation tools like Hubspot or Marketo.

P6. Social

Be a consistent, respected publisher and influencer across various Social Networks.

P7. Mobile

Develop and promote successful mobile apps.

Level 6: Black Belt

Advanced Level 2

Black belts are typically sought after industry experts, who frequent conference circuits and lead agencies, as well as digital marketing departments. Anyone truly at this level is more than qualified for some kind of leadership role. Most black belts focus largely on Modes 1-4 (Ideation, ROI, Strategy and People). They know how to build teams, scale marketing programs, pitch and win new business and communicate a project's vision.

There are two other styles of black belt, that don't seek leadership positions, because they don't enjoy or aren't skilled at managing others. They are just very good at what they do, with a particular skill set that is hard to match. This group thrives as either independent contractors or high-level implementation tacticians within a corporation.

Examples of Black Belts by Angle:

L6-A1) Industry's Top Bloggers and Account Directors of Award-Winning Advertising Campaigns.

L6-A2) Reputable Cinematographers, Photographers and Award-Winning Web Designers.

L6-A3) Coders and System Architects behind the leading mobile apps and Social Networks.

L6-A4) CEOs and COOs of Fortune 500 companies, as well as successful SMBs and startups.

L6-A5) CFOs and Finance Managers across top companies, ad agencies and marketing departments.

L6-A6) Partners at top Silicon Valley law firms; as well as in-house Counsel at large agencies.

L6-A7) Proven Venture Capitalists and Angel Investors.

Consummate and proven professionals, Black Belts are able to...

P1. Content

Self-actualize, discover, coach or promote topnotch authors, filmmakers, photographers, and other content producers.

P2. UX

Assemble, manage inspire and deploy award-winning web development teams; Architect scalable and complex web builds.

P3. Search

Instill SEO culture and cross-channel integration; Recruit and train skilled SEO technicians; Author at least five (5) major SEO ROI success stories.

P4. Media

Create (at least 5) scalable, fully integrated and positive ROI campaigns in competitive industries and multiple markets.

P5. CRM

Build, train and deploy cross-functional CRM teams, including active response support and customer service centers.

P6. Social

Innovate and develop popular Social plugins, buzz generating campaigns and brand awareness raising concepts.

P7. Mobile

Innovate and develop new mobile platforms, strategies and app categories.

Level 7: Blue Belt

Blue Samurais are rare beings. These game-changing entrepreneurs and executives are pure geniuses, proven at the highest levels. Think Bruce Lee, Steve Jobs, Michael Jordan - masters of their craft. Blue belts are the creators of the tech and marketing industries, who understand how to navigate and excel in these worlds better than anyone. They reside inside the Temples of Digital Knowledge, where the Pillars represent Truth and Blue Samurais are the Prophets. Blue belts represent the gold standard and the ideal that all marketers aspire to. In reality, only 1% of Samurais attain this status. Nonetheless, we can all learn a great deal from them. They are simply the best at what they do.

On a related note, the name of my digital marketing agency, Blueliner, represents this pinnacle of knowledge; the relevant image being of a Samurai holding that blue belt up right, as the standard to which all marketers aspire (Page 10 illustrates this). I only hire people who I feel want to reach this level, even if they never do - the aspiration and model gives them the fire to succeed.

Exercise:

Evaluate two businesses, where you know at least one iconic - Blue Samurai-type leader - works, that you feel do a fantastic job of being of being innovative and game changing. What attributes make you think they really are? Compare your business to each of these businesses and create a list of both similarities and differences. How would you - and your company - have to evolve in order to put your company on that same path? Envision what you would have to sacrifice and do to become a Blue Samurai.

Blue Belts do the following and much more...

P1. Content

Create mega-publishing enterprise or release. [Members include Ariana Huffington, Deepak Chopra, Bono, Sting, Steven Spielberg, J.K. Rowling, J.R.R. Tolkien and Howard Stern].

P2. UX

Launch game-changing tech firms and products. [Members include Bill Gates, Larry Ellison and Jonathan Gay (Creator of Flash)].

P3. Search

Spearhead a whole new industry. [Members include Larry Paige, Sergey Brin and Matt Cutts (all of Google)].

P4. Media

Innovate and Master Online Ad platforms. [Members include Jerry Yang (Yahoo Founder) and Bill Gross (GoTo Founder)].

P5. CRM

Spawn a new communications management industry. [Members include Marc Benioff and Parker Harris (Salesforce.com Founders) and Josh James (DOMO and Overture Founder)].

P6. Social

Reinvent Social Media. [Members include Mark Zuckerberg and Langley Steinert (Co-Founder of TripAdvisor)].

P7. Mobile

Pioneer the Smartphone movement. [Members include the iconic Steve Jobs and Jack Dorsey (Square and Twitter Founder)].

Pyramids
of knowledge
by Level & Angle

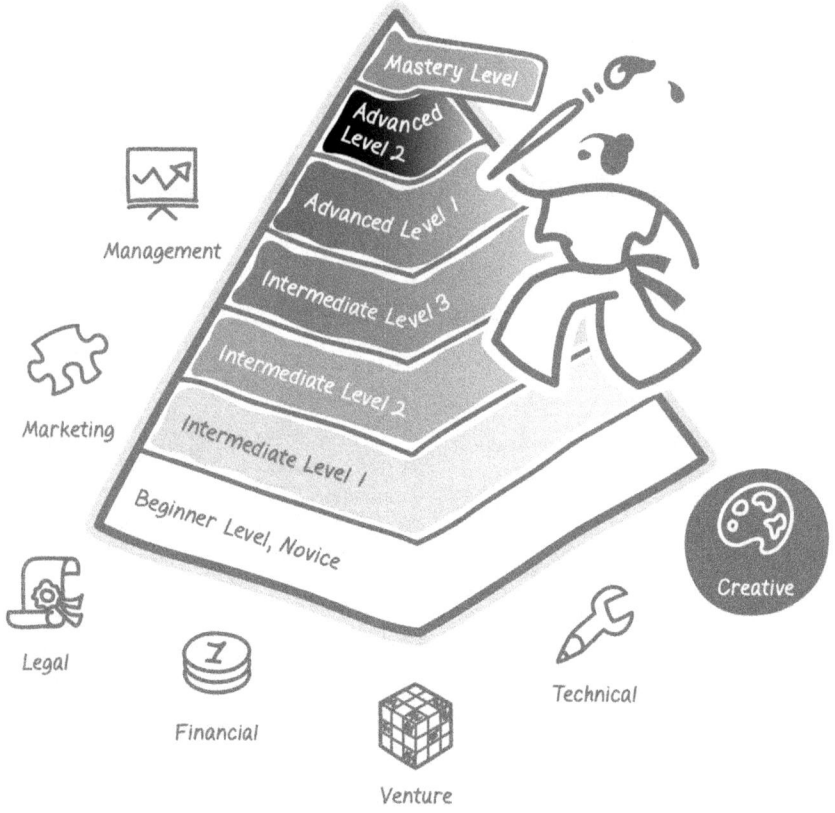

Mastery Level

Advanced Level 2

Advanced Level 1

Intermediate Level 3

Intermediate Level 2

Intermediate Level 1

Beginner Level, Novice

Management

Marketing

Legal

Financial

Venture

Technical

Creative

The Pyramids of Knowledge represent the Samurai's ascension through the various skill levels of the multi-dimensional, digital marketing universe. This is another dynamic infographic-like tool which can be applied in a number of ways, for example to evaluate individuals, teams, products and campaigns. Most importantly, the Pyramids give us an appreciation for the vastness of information, approaches and tactics that exist in this field, as well as a visual roadmap for how we can progress along the most suitable tracks given our current starting point.

The Pyramids of Knowledge are created by crossing the 3rd and 4th Dimensions (Angles and Levels). If the 49er Matrix is the virtual chessboard, then the Pyramids turn that board into a 4-Dimensional battle field. Pyramids generally have seven different positions and sizes (outlined on Pages 104-105), which represent who is being evaluated, and in what domain of knowledge.

As is the case with any mature system, the further you move towards the top, the less people exist at that level. Similar to the traditional dojo system of training, those who train thoroughly progress faster. Many others fall off or stagnate.

The 7 Pillars model provides a clear and consistent evaluation system of skill set and level. In the karate world, when dojos come together at tournaments, oftentimes lower belts from a particular dojo will prevail over higher ranking belts from another. This happens because the true essence of what a new level entails is not always grasped or properly taught, even by those wearing advanced colors. 7 Pillars takes an objective approach towards evaluations and promotions (to new Levels), valuing each aspirant's experience, education, ethics and most importantly, actual results in the field of work.

D3 D4

How To Use The Pyramids

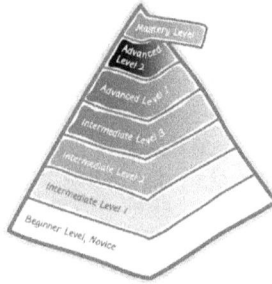

1)

At the highest level, there is one Pyramid that represents the whole field. Envision it as a big Pyramid on top of the 49er Matrix. This can be used to demonstrate your overall knowledge level as a Digital Marketer.

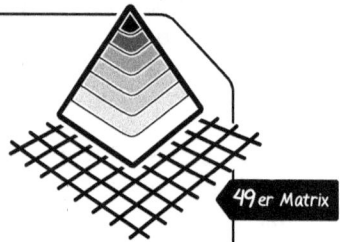

49er Matrix

2)

Take that model to an even broader level by applying the Pyramid to Integrated Marketing, which includes 12 Pillars.

3)

Going deeper, Pyramids can sit on top of each Pillar or Mode, for example to evaluate someone in SEO we would have a Pyramid on top of the 3rd Pillar.

P3 Search

4)

Getting to a more granular level, each Pyramid can sit on top of a Matrix Block, of which there are generally 49. Here we are evaluating a more particular area, such as "Search Marketing Strategy" or "Online Media Budgeting" skills.

P3 / M3   P4 / M2

5)

Drilling down one level deeper, we can take this visual evaluation tool to very particular tactics or scenarios that operate within different Pillars or Modes; for example, not just SEO, but specifically, Technical SEO or Link Building.

6)

Pyramids can be applied to the 5th Dimension (Markets) to evaluate experience in relation to demographic targets.

7)

Pyramids can be applied to the 6th Dimension (Industries) to understand whether someone has a relevant background.

D3   D4

Target Your Audience

Markets
Segmentation

Demo
Filters

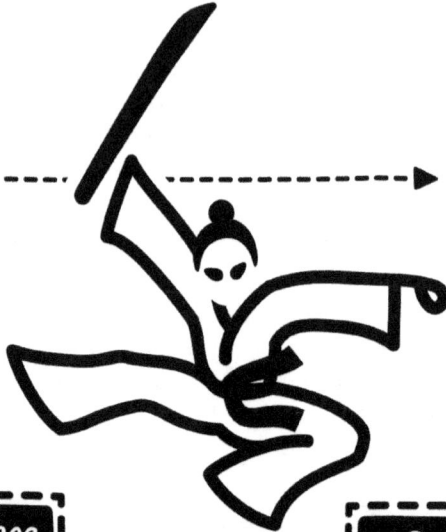

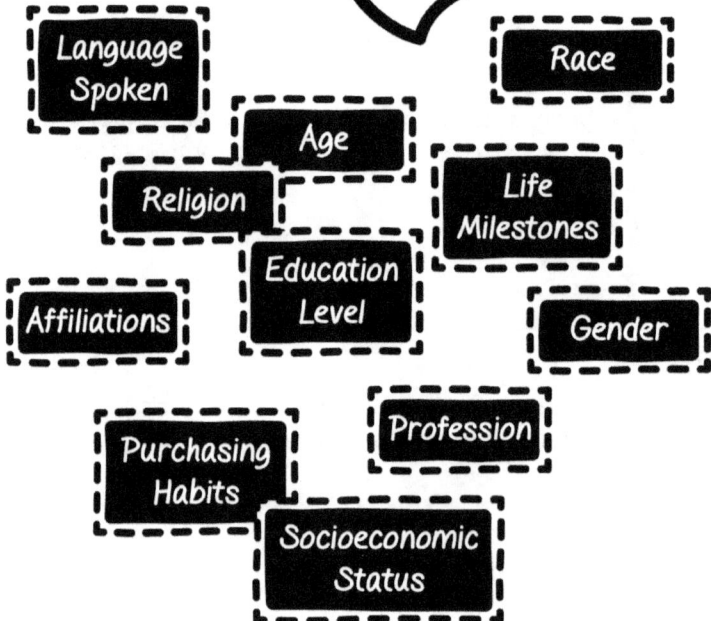

Language
Spoken

Race

Age

Religion

Life
Milestones

Affiliations

Education
Level

Gender

Purchasing
Habits

Profession

Socioeconomic
Status

Dimension 5:

Markets (Geos, Demos & Psych)

Markets (D5) include the vast field of the segmentation and targeting of various audiences amidst the global marketplace (i.e. essentially the 7+ billion people that we currently have on Planet Earth). Unless you are Coca-Cola, you cannot target the whole world. From 7 billion individuals, companies hone in on their target markets by three general methods: **1)** Geography or Location, **2)** Demographics or Consumer Profiles, and **3)** Psychographics or Customer Lifestyle & Behavior. Effective audience segmentation leads to better personalization and a more satisfying user experience with brands.

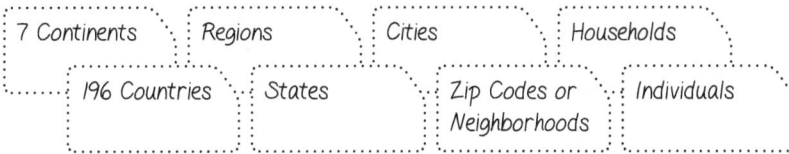

7 Continents	Regions	Cities	Households
196 Countries	States	Zip Codes or Neighborhoods	Individuals

Demo Filter:

- Age
- Gender
- Language Spoken
- Race
- Religion
- Socioeconomic Status
- Education Level
- Profession
- Affiliations (i.e. Hobbies, Sports, Interests)
- Purchasing Habits
- Life Milestones (i.e. Getting Married, Having a Baby, Graduation)

Transcending
Specificity

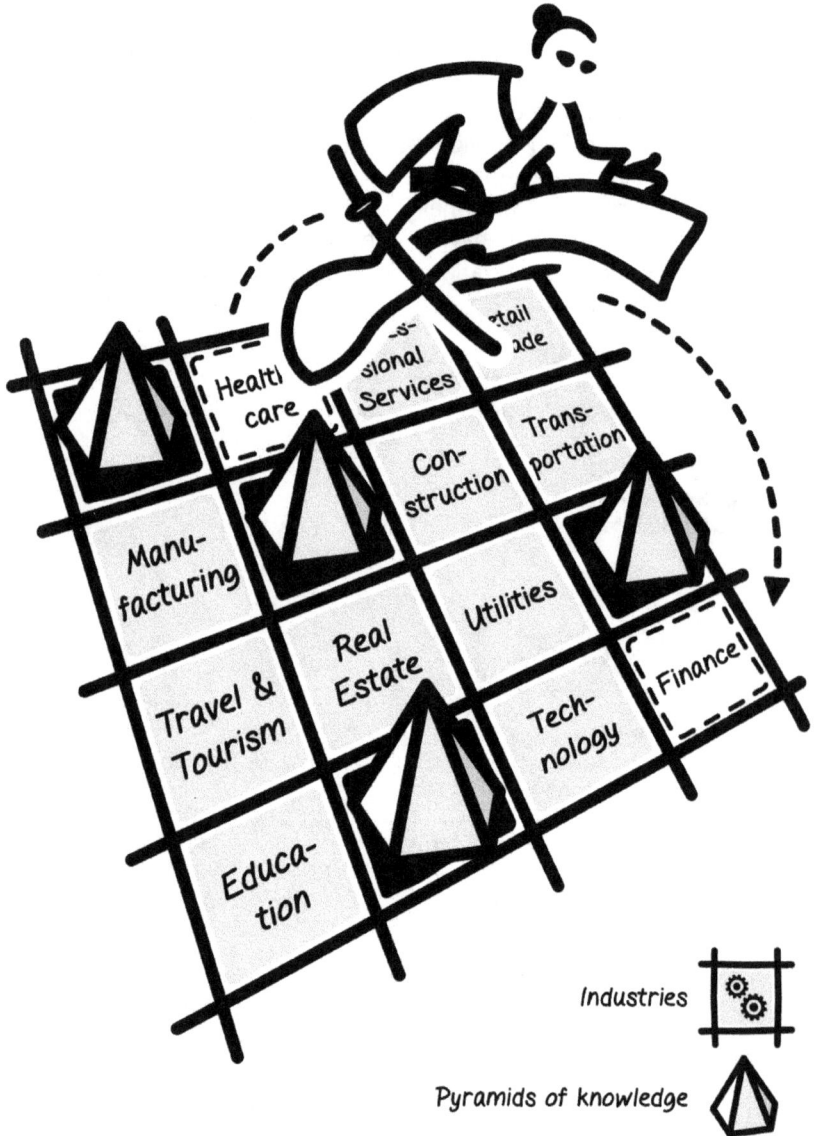

Health care

sional Services

tail ade

Trans-portation

Con-struction

Manu-facturing

Utilities

Real Estate

Travel & Tourism

Tech-nology

Finance

Educa-tion

Industries

Pyramids of knowledge

Dimension 6:

Industries

I believe that great marketing transcends industry-specific nuances. If you are a strong media buyer or copywriter in Healthcare for example, you should be able to port that skill set over to a Financial Services account. 7 Pillars best practices are generally agnostic and hold their value across the board. That being said, there are particulars including terminology, tone, trends, regulations and a power structure (i.e. politics), within each industry that take time to get in sync with. The failure to study and comply with this domain knowledge can be detrimental to a company and its marketing.

The number of Industries (D6) can range from 30 to over 100, depending on whose list you use and how granular you get. Most top level industries have five or more sub-sectors; so the filtration and associated potential for specialization goes very deep. As it relates to marketers, we must strike a balance between finding our niche industries that inspire us and maintaining perspective on big picture, transcendental marketing principles. For my agency – Blueliner – we have serviced clients in almost every industry since 2001. My philosophy has been to remain agnostic, in general, while building our teams around several core industries where we have had the most success (i.e. Travel & Tourism, Healthcare, Startups).

Some industries change a lot faster than others and are therefore more open to cutting edge marketing ideas. Highly regulated industries, such as Healthcare and Financial Services, tend to be conservative and therefore less cutting edge in certain areas of marketing. The advantage of this is that it narrows down the scope of possible Strategies (M3) and time required to Brainstorm (M1) ideas. The ROI (M2) models are well-known so benchmarks are pre-defined. Conversely, tech and media startups have much less structure, restrictions and benchmarks in place, which opens far more creative doors and opportunities for innovation.

The Past   The Future

p1	p2	p3	p4	p5		p7
Content	Design	Search	Media	CRM	Social **PILLAR 6**	Mobile

m1 Brainstorming

m2 ROI

m3 Strategy

m4 People

m5 Tools

m6 Execution

m7 Analytics

p6	m7	Level 7		
Social	Analytics	Mastery		Julie

(Task: Use the 49er Matrix to evaluate your past performance and to map out your future goals in one or several subsections of the marketing ecosystem.

Analytics X Social	Past Year	Future Goals
# of Blog Posts		
# of Social Media accounts		
# of Active Twitter Followers		
# of Facebook Fans		
Engagements (Likes/Shares/Mentions)		
# of Hours Invested		
Budgets Managed		

Dimension 7:
Time [Eras]

In simplest terms, D7 (Time) can be broken down into Past, Present and Future. It's easy to forget that today's most indispensable tools didn't exist until fairly recently. Before 2010, most people didn't have smartphones and mobile apps. The Internet itself is less than 25 years old! Every 5 years is like an entirely new Era, with new players, rules and requisite survival skills. Change is constant and the pace of it is ever-increasing. As marketers, D7 helps us organize our goals, teams, campaigns and knowledge base around specific periods of time, be it quarterly, annually or multi-yearly. You also need to know how long things take to get done - which brings back CP1 - Time Mastery and self-knowledge. In producing business plans, timelines are paramount - covering the Past (Company & Management History), Present (Current Ideas & Status), and Future (Capital Needs & Goals).

This is the outermost Dimension because it puts everything in perspective. As a digital marketer, your comprehension of history and trends will put you ahead of the curve, giving you the awareness to help your clients and partners navigate uncertainty and opportunity. Tactics that work today won't be en vogue or work the same way tomorrow. For example, an entire segment of marketers and brands hold their collective breath every time Google's algorithm changes in the SEO world. In this environment, billions of dollars are at stake and the calling card for success is adaptability.

"Those who do not learn from history are bound to repeat it!"

How do we keep the principles of Dimension 7 alive in our work? I recommend maintaining a clear vision (ideally, a 5 year plan), for your own career and whatever companies you have a stake in. Being goal-oriented, reading up on trends, experimenting with new ideas and essentially not allowing your knowledge to get stale, are the keys to ensuring that Time (D7) remains on your side!

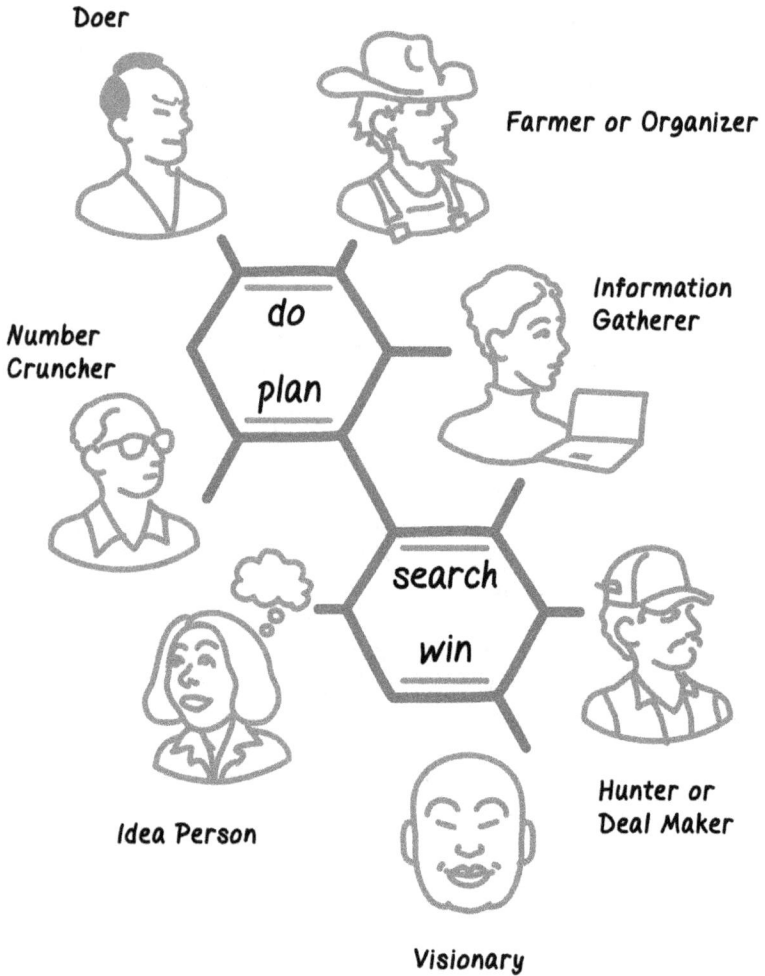

Chemistry
is important

Doer

Farmer or Organizer

Information
Gatherer

Number
Cruncher

do

plan

search

win

Idea Person

Hunter or
Deal Maker

Visionary

The 7 Marketing Personality Types (MPT)

"Know Thyself". One of the keys to success in life, and for one to achieve happiness, is knowing who you are. The same goes for your marketing career. The Marketing Personality Types (MPTs) represent a subset of Mode 4 (People). From over twenty years of working with all types of characters, I have distilled the archetypes down to, you guessed it, 7 distinct MPTs.

Everyone has some percentage of all 7 qualities in varying degrees. It is critical to have a general sense for what areas you (and your collaborators) are strongest in and most aligned with. This is analogues to our Astrological make-up, whereby we have different degrees of all the planets and horoscope signs operating through us. There are also different levels of each quality. For example, an L1 (White Belt) Farmer (one of the MPTs) can be a top-notch Administrative Assistant, keeping things in order; whereas, an L7 (Blue Belt) Farmer can be a great CEO or General Manager of a big group of people.

While most people have specific tendencies towards one MPT, some are adaptable and take on different roles within different groups, depending on the makeup of that group – which is a great quality.

Aside from our core MPTs, individuals have other qualities (Tendency Scales), which should be understood, especially by managers who have to create cultures and build cohesive teams. Here are some Tendency Scales worthy of noting when it comes to classifying individuals:

> Teaching vs. Learning

> Doing vs. Thinking/Planning vs. Analyzing

> Detail (Micro) vs. Big Picture (Macro) Oriented

> Introvert (Independent) vs. Extrovert (Social)

> Self-Focused vs. Team Oriented (even if introvert-ed, one can be for the team cause; as can be seen with extroversion)

MPTI:

Number Cruncher

Common Roles:

CFO, Accountant, Financial Analyst, Programmer, Statistician, Analytics Specialist.

A close relative of ROI (Mode 2) and Financial (Angle 6), the Number Cruncher (NC) views the business world through the lens of Excel spreadsheets. Every marketing team needs at least one math and/or coding whiz to bring a quantitative perspective to the table. NCs bring an unbiased, scientific mentality to the evaluation of marketing campaigns, evaluating tactics on their ROI and not their cool factor. Softer metrics, like brand awareness and customer satisfaction, while not as appealing to the NC, can also carry some weight as long as they connect to the bottom line.

As with all Types, it is important for the NC not to be one-dimensional, and instead to diversify by adding at least one or two more perspectives to his or her marketing arsenal. Otherwise, they risk becoming type casted as "uncreative" and "too rigid." It is similar to the curse of a skeptical scientist who refuses to accept possibilities that are unproven in formal lab tests. On the other hand, if NCs add some creative and complementary strategy skills to their arsenal, they can become some of the most powerful marketers in the room.

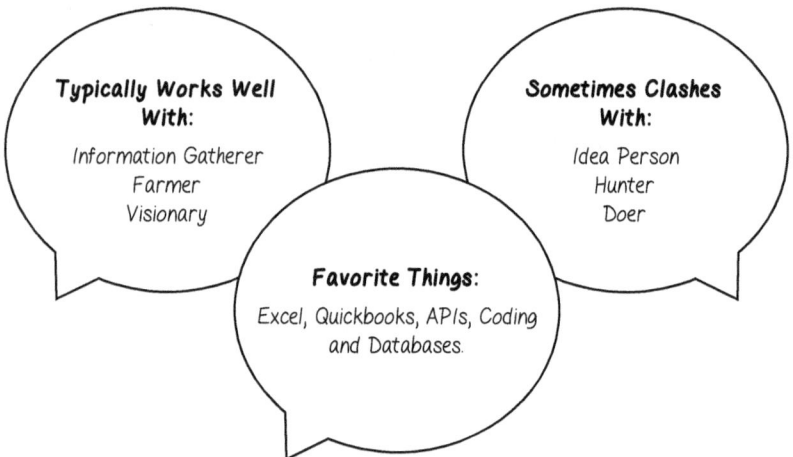

Typically Works Well With:

Information Gatherer
Farmer
Visionary

Sometimes Clashes With:

Idea Person
Hunter
Doer

Favorite Things:

Excel, Quickbooks, APIs, Coding and Databases.

MPT2:

Information Gatherer

As a close relative of Brainstorming (Mode 1), Strategy (Mode 3), Business Intelligence (Core Principle 5) and Research (Angle 4), the Information Gatherer (IG) believes in the power of data. They are the fastest and most dynamic web crawlers around, and seem to know how to find information that the rest of us didn't think was possible to locate. They are masters of the SWOT analysis and can construct a PowerPoint deck like nobody's business. IGs make for great Business Analysts. With market research as their core trade, oftentimes IGs can over-analyze and suffer from Analysis Paralysis. If this becomes a trend, it can prevent them from being decisive and becoming strong Project Managers. They generally hesitate to move forward based on informed intuition and without an airtight plan.

The IG can be a friend or foe to other types based on how well they support the needs of the other functions (i.e. by providing useful sales-related research that helps close deals). Combining IG traits with NC quant skills can yield powerful, truly scientific marketing results. Information gathering can be a lost art amidst the more sexy Marketing Personality Types. With that being said, there has never been a better time for them with the rapidly expanding, information rich Internet being as open and accessible as ever.

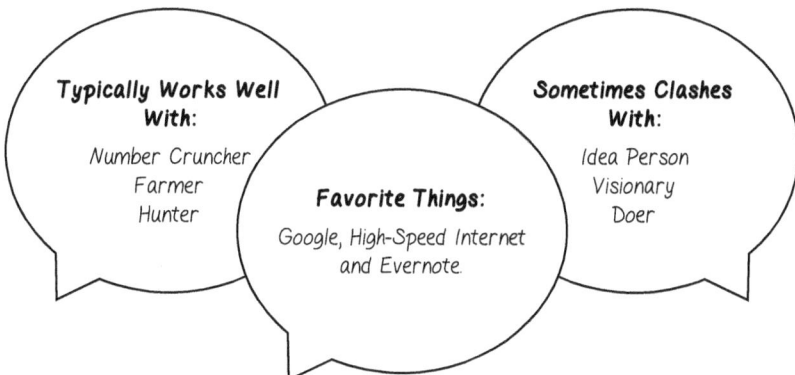

Typically Works Well With:

Number Cruncher
Farmer
Hunter

Favorite Things:

Google, High-Speed Internet and Evernote.

Sometimes Clashes With:

Idea Person
Visionary
Doer

MPT3:

Hunter

Common Roles:

Sales, Business Development, Strategic Dealmaker, M&A, Presentation Specialist, Closer.

The Hunter is actually rooted in one of the Traditional Pillars (tP5 Sales) and reflects a character that is aggressive, proactive and interactive. Good hunters know how to go out and engage decision makers, and convince them to decide in their favor. They don't necessarily need the backing of research and numbers but they do need to know how to utilize that supporting data well when it is available to them. Organizing and managing projects is not their forte. If put in this position, Hunters often miss the finer details, even if it is something they have promised to a client.

The Hunter can become a very one-sided personality type if not tempered by other energies. Selling ideas and projects that are not practical or budgeted properly only leads to disappointment all-around in the end. On the flipside, when it is time to motivate a team, an audience or a group of shareholders, no MPT short of the Visionary is more charming and convincing than a well-trained Hunter.

Typically Works Well With:

Information Gatherer
Idea Person
Visionary

Sometimes Clashes With:

Number Cruncher
Farmer
Doer

Favorite Things:

Frequent Flyer miles, Trade Shows, LinkedIn and a healthy T&E (Entertainment) budget.

MPT4:

Farmer

While Hunters bring in the catch of the day, Farmers have to prepare it for the feast. Closely related to the Management Angle (A5), Farmers do just that, manage projects. Good Farmers are generally well-grounded, low key, detail oriented and risk averse. They have their feet on the ground and appreciate structure, even if they're able to be productive in less structured environments (it is a huge plus if they have this flexibility). If Farmers are not given the proper support and resources, they may struggle, especially if their management capabilities are not matched by at least some level of "hands on" implementation skills.

Common Roles:

Manager, General Manager, P.M, Supervisor, Coordinator, Organizer.

Farmers aren't typically the most social creatures but they know how to interact and get along well enough on a work-level to be productive in groups.

Typically Works Well With:

Information Gatherer
Number Cruncher
Doer

Favorite Things:

Spreadsheets, Approved Budgets and Project Management Software.

Sometimes Clashes With:

Idea Person
Visionary
Hunter

MPT5:

Idea Person

The Idea Man or Woman (IM or IW) is a spark plug and source of creative energy that shines in the early stages of a project, and Mode 1 (Brainstorming). They can be zany, charismatic characters and potentially company leaders (i.e. aspiring visionaries). They generally do not like being constricted or controlled and tend to function better in more open, (non-corporate) creative environments. They have no regard for defining or managing a project's scope. In their minds, everything is possible, even if there is a limited budget.

IMs don't care about data and can fall asleep when Number Crunchers or Farmers are presenting their case. They can drive others up the wall with their tangential thinking and non-stop ideation process. The strong mental energy possessed by an IM needs to be balanced, either within or by their team, with more grounded types that can focus on actually manifesting and exploring the feasibility of those ideas.

The Doer said to the Idea Man; "1% Inspiration, 99% Perspiration. Now let's get back to work!". The IM then replied; "Every great company and marketing campaign started with an idea. Work without vision is aimless! Balance is the key".

Typically Works Well With:

Information Gatherer
Visionary
Hunter

Sometimes Clashes With:

Number Cruncher
Doer
Farmer

Favorite Things:

Whiteboard Walls, Mood Boards, Spontaneous Brainstorming Sessions, and Active Collaborators.

MPT6:
Doer

Nike's "Just Do It" is the motto of the Doer, an action-oriented character who likes to live in Mode 6 (Execution). This type is the most resourceful and is not afraid to learn new things. The Doer is a workhorse, who is not particularly fond of meetings, hierarchy and bureaucracy. They just want to know their tasks, and be given the space to do them in peace. They are not satisfied until things are done and done well.

Common Roles:

Man or Woman of Action, the ones who dig in and do; Resourceful, Independent, non-Managers.

Doers get "wired in" like the Social Network movie and resent those who derail them from being in the zone. Knocking out tasks reduces their anxiety and almost becomes an addiction. This focused and grounded type of marketer gets irritated by the more abstract thinkers among us, such as Idea Men and Visionaries. However, a strong Visionary knows how to partner up with Doers and channel their skills productively. Information Gatherers can also annoy Doers because of the IG's hesitation to dive into tasks until they have supporting data.

Typically Works Well With:

Farmer
Number Cruncher
Visionary

Sometimes Clashes With:

Information Gatherer
Idea Person
Hunter

Favorite Things:

Canceled Meetings, Free Airport WiFi, Morning Coffee and Quiet Workspaces.

MPT7:

Visionary

Common Roles:

Leader, Chief Strategist, Boss, CEO, President, Aura about him/her. The most powerful, and must be high level at 3 or more of the prior types.

The Visionary is the most evolved of all MPTs. They always seem one step ahead of the game. Their clear-sighted comprehension of particular business problems and optimal solutions, when matched by an ability to articulate that vision, yields unparalleled potential. They see the big picture better than anyone, and while well aware of their necessity, rarely fret about the details. These mission-driven people (i.e. Mark Zuckerberg and Bill Gates) learn very quickly that they are the smartest people in the room, and often take the Venture Angle (A7), blazing new trails of innovation (Core Principle 4). They don't aspire to master some type of service or set of tactics; they want to recreate the game itself.

Depending on the sensitivity level of the Visionary, the team built around them must be able to feed off of their energy and not vice versa. A Visionary has no place taking direction from Farmers or Hunters, which will quickly stifle their creativity. In a sense, a Visionary is an evolved form of several other types combined, possibly even all. Evolved and strong Visionaries tend to attract all kinds of talent as well as less talented people, who just sometimes feed off of their energy. They know how to manage their energy and harness the collective knowledge of their teams, respecting the need for each MPT in a balanced and holistic marketing operation.

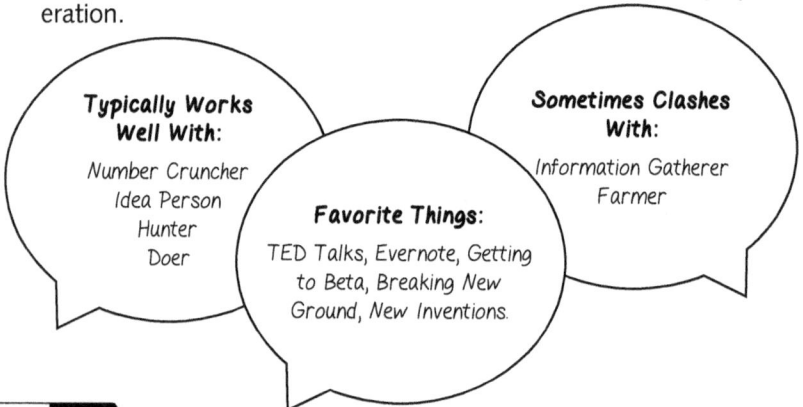

Typically Works Well With:

Number Cruncher
Idea Person
Hunter
Doer

Favorite Things:

TED Talks, Evernote, Getting to Beta, Breaking New Ground, New Inventions.

Sometimes Clashes With:

Information Gatherer
Farmer

Know Your Best Time of Day!

Early Bird

Night Owl

While identifying your major and minor MPT, it is also important to know if you are an "Early Bird" or a "Night Owl." If you are the type of person who wakes up at the crack of dawn to attack the day, you're probably an Early Bird. You're most productive and at your sharpest in the beginning of the day.

Night Owls are exactly the opposite. They are most effective plugging away in a dark room amidst the glow of a computer screen. They can function on little sleep and the unstructured freedom of the night. Being a Night Owl is definitely going against the grain of the formal corporate world - but times are changing, and we are discovering that more people would prefer this lifestyle and are more productive if given the freedom to work in their peek state.

In order for a team to meld efficiently and seamlessly, it is crucial for you to know and be cognizant of when you and everyone else around you are most productive. The key is to be flexible when it comes to time management, meeting schedules and communication. While everyone has to be adaptable to working outside of their peek productive zone, forcing a square peg into a round hole never works out in the long run.

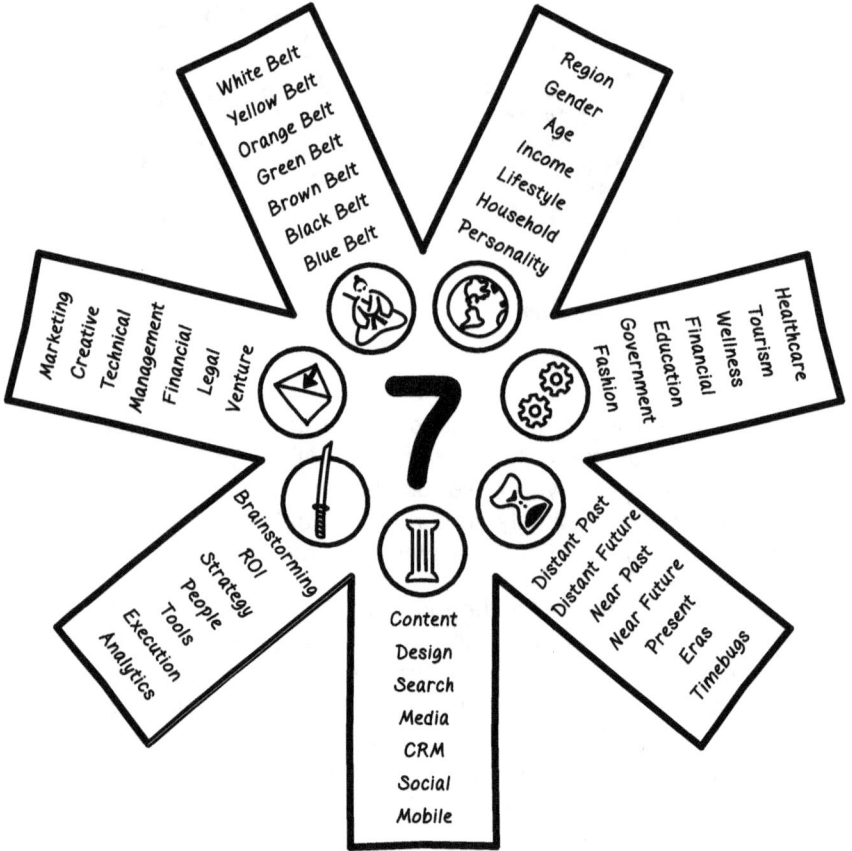

White Belt
Yellow Belt
Orange Belt
Green Belt
Brown Belt
Black Belt
Blue Belt

Region
Gender
Age
Income
Lifestyle
Household
Personality

Marketing
Creative
Technical
Management
Financial
Legal
Venture

Healthcare
Tourism
Wellness
Financial
Education
Government
Fashion

Brainstorming
ROI
Strategy
People
Tools
Execution
Analytics

Content
Design
Search
Media
CRM
Social
Mobile

Distant Past
Distant Future
Near Past
Near Future
Present
Eras
Timebugs

7

Conclusion & Follow-Ups

I hope that you have enjoyed this introduction to 7 Pillars - now it's time to put what you've learned into practice! This is not a theoretical framework, but an actionable, practical guide to marketing that can be applied by and for individuals, companies, campaigns, websites, marketing plans and budgets.

I leave you with four quick tips, to aid your path towards marketing excellence.

1) **FRESH.** I encourage you to stay fresh in your practice and sustain a flexible approach towards learning. There is a lot to learn in this rapidly changing field which is precisely why you should use a system that helps organize your knowledge, at whatever level you stand.

2) FOCUS. Do not get overwhelmed and do not overestimate yourself just to impress others or boost your resume. This always backfires and does not serve you. Pick 2-3 areas to keep up on and don't try to take on too much at once.

3) MACRO. Keep the Big Picture in Mind. Develop a macro-micro habit of getting into details and then coming back out from the weeds to see the bigger picture.

4) **BASICS.** Don't get too caught up in the newest marketing trends. We all want to keep up with the latest in our respective fields but to be honest, 90% of the basics of marketing aren't done well, which on a principal level, has not changed all that much. In a karate dojo, students always start with basic techniques and build up from there.

I hope that this will be just the first step in your journey with 7 Pillars. The framework is actively unfolding and evolving as we speak. All of the latest resources, apps, events, case studies, templates and news about 7 Pillars is available on the website *www.7pillarsdigital.com*. See you out there, in the Digital Universe!

About 7 Pillars of Digital Marketing Academy

The 7 Pillars of Digital Marketing Academy, LLC is an original education content publisher and center of learning - featuring both classroom and online courses - for those who aspire to excellence in the fields of marketing and Internet technology. The 7 Pillars system is based on the experience of industry veterans, specifically digital marketers and technologists from Blueliner Marketing, LLC, a global, digital agency that was founded by Arman Rousta and Dali Singh in 2001. 7 Pillars is being incubated in b.labs, Blueliner's innovation lab based in Jersey City.

7 Pillars Academy educates individuals and companies, to:

1) Increase digital IQ and keep up the latest digital strategies;

2) Learn how to evaluate individual aptitude for being a successful marketer, and find the right track and skill mix to develop;

3) Manage marketing campaigns efficiently, within a strong ROI and KPI-driven system.

Check out our latest offerings at ***7pillarsdma.com.***

About The Author

A serial entrepreneur, Arman has built several successful companies, including Blueliner, Ajustco, 401kid and Exeter Technologies. He created this 7 Pillars system, which has been utilized to drive millions of dollars in marketing ROI, by Fortune 500 companies, startups, non-profits and governments worldwide. He is also a time mastery expert, teaching other entrepreneurs and business leaders about holistic life and time management through another system that he developed, called Timebug.

Arman co-invented a best-selling, patented safety product called Park-Zone, that has sold millions of units since its launch in 1998.

Arman Co-Founded Ajustco, a product development company, which – with Blueliner's help and the 7 Pillars methodology – sells an award-winning, also patented innovation across worldwide hardware stores, including Home Depot.

Arman gives talks and training on business, leadership, marketing and time & life management, throughout the world.

Arman graduated from Columbia, where he was an Academic All-Ivy League soccer player. A native New Yorker – born and raised in Staten Island – he now resides in Jersey City, NJ.

Arman's personal blog is available at *www.armanrousta.com*.

Glossary

7 Core Principles – The seven primary, defining characteristics of the 7 Pillars methodology, including Time Management, ROI (Goal Driven), Holistic, Innovation Driven, Business Intelligence, Active Knowledge Sharing and Organic & Agile Workflow.

7 Dimensions – The master filtration system of marketing practices, including the 7 Pillars, 7 Modes, 7 Levels, 7 Angles, Markets, Industries and Time (Eras).

7 Marketing Personality Types – A subset of Mode 4 (People), the Marketing Personality Types (MPTs) representing the archetypes of personalities that people have while working in the marketing world. Everyone has some percentage of all 7 qualities, to varying degrees.

7 Modes of Marketing – The stages that are vital to almost every Marketing process or project including Brainstorming, ROI, Strategy, People, Tools, Execution and Analytics. The term "modes" makes more sense as the official distinction because "stages" often can and do occur out of sequence.

7 Pillars of Digital Marketing – The name given to the first (and broadest) Dimension of the system consisting of Content, Design, Search, Media, CRM, Social and Mobile.

7 Pillars of Traditional Marketing – The roots of the Marketing field consisting of traditionally 'offline' aspects including Content, Branding, Advertising, PR, Sales, Event Marketing and Direct Marketing.

7 Levels – 7 Pillars breaks things down using 7 Levels of skill (of the individual) and the corresponding difficulty (of the task). Marketing practitioners progress in their ability at particular Pillars throughout their careers – from beginner level, through intermediate and all the way to advanced and mastery.

7 Angles – If you envision the 7 Pillars as 7 Pyramids, where the pinnacle represents the culmination of knowledge, the Angles are the sides of the Pyramids. Individuals ascend the Pyramids using different tracks or aspects of a particular body of knowledge.

12 Pillars of Integrated Marketing – The Digital Marketing (7) and Traditional Marketing (7) Pillar systems combine to make 12 Pillars of Integrated Marketing (7+7=14, 14-2=12) because two Pillars on each 'side' (i.e. Content and Advertising) combine into one.

49er Matrix – The 49er Matrix is a visual tool, a template for Marketing Audits and Plans for individuals, companies, agencies, campaigns, websites and products. It can be thought of as a 7-Dimensional Chess Board, upon which we play out the strategic game of Marketing. The first two dimensions (7 Pillars x 7 Modes) generate 49 blocks, each of which contains specific best practices and prompts important marketing questions.

A/B Testing – A type of marketing research where variable elements are changed in a control scenario (e.g. Facebook ad) in order to determine the most effective solution for the final marketing strategy (e.g. most click throughs).

Above the Fold – The visible portion of the webpage without scrolling down.

Accelerometer – An instrument for measuring acceleration, typically found in most mobile devices nowadays. Examples of platforms that use the function include Snapchat, which captures the speed you are travelling when taking an image (don't drive and Snap!!).

Adaptive Design – A concept of web design whereby your website is optimized for viewability on several device types through the use of a predefined set of layout sizes based on screen dimensions. Adaptive is similar to Responsive Design.

Advertising – The profession or activity of relaying communications to an audience in order to persuade them to purchase your commercial product or service.

Affiliate Marketing – The sharing of revenue between online publishers/salespeople and online advertisers/merchants, whereby return is based on performance metrics including clicks, sales, registrations etc.

Agency (Marketing) – A service-based business that creates, plans, and executes marketing strategies for its clients.

Agency Fees – The service free for marketing agencies.

Analytics – The statistical analysis of data in order to optimize the performance of a website, marketing campaign etc.

Animation – A simulation of movement that is created by displaying a series of pictures or frames in varying positions.

API – An acronym for 'Application Programming Interface' that refers to a set of protocols and tools for building software applications. In Marketing, these are most commonly used to pull information from external sources (i.e. Facebook feeds).

App – A self-contained piece of software or program designed to fulfill a particular purpose. It is downloaded by a user to a device, most commonly on mobile.

App Development – The entire process of developing an app from concept to completion, most commonly for the iOS or Android operating systems.

App Fatigue – The experience of users becoming overwhelmed by choice as the number of similar apps on the market increases. This adversely affects the potential adoption rate for your app.

Agile Workflow – A less restrictive, more 'free-flowing' model of how necessary tasks for a project or campaign are completed. This differs from a more traditional model, in that tasks and actions do not necessarily have to occur in sequential order or at defined times and locations.

Audience – Your audience is the population to which you are targeting for a campaign, strategy, communication or advertisement with call-to-actions.

Audience Segmentation – This is the process of dividing the target audience into subgroups based on defined criterion such as demographics, psychographics and geographics. This is a key component of Pillar 5 (CRM).

Automation – Marketing automation uses software and technologies to effectively use multiple channels at once (i.e. email, social media) to automate repeating tasks. This is another key part of CRM (P5), related to Lead Nurturing.

Banner Ads – Image-based ads used to promote a brand, product or service and/or to drive traffic from the host website to the advertiser's website.

Bing – A web search engine created and operated by Microsoft and holds approximately 20% share of the search market in 2015.

Blog(s) – (n) A continually updated website or web page generally on a specialized topic. (v) To 'blog' about something also means to create and publish a blog entry on that subject.

Blog Topics – The subject or theme about which a blog entry is written.

Bounce Rate – The percentage of visitors to a particular website who, after viewing only one page on the site, navigate away.

Boosted Post – Social media content (i.e. Facebook) that increases audience size through the payment of a fee by the company or agency who posted the content to the platform provider.

Brand / Branding – The differentiation of a company, product or service based on particular qualities, features, aspects or benefits. Both a noun and a verb, branding can be used to describe the identity of a company and their products or services. It is also the act of visually displaying a company's logo on something for recognition and differentiation.

Brand Awareness – The extent to which consumers recognize the image or distinctive qualities of a particular brand of goods or services.

Brand Guidelines – A document or set of procedures that outlines how brands should communicate with it's consumers and target market. It generally includes a logo, taglines, colors, packaging, tone of voice, communication strategy and much more.

Brainstorming – A Mode (M1) that involves gathering and generating all types of ideas and information, generally more practiced during the Discovery Phase of a project or campaign.

Brochures – A small magazine or book containing visuals and information about a company, product or service.

Budget – An estimate and plan of the financial goals associated with the successful execution and running of a particular marketing strategy, project or campaign.

Budget Allocation / Budgeting – The act of setting forward looking, ROI-focused goals and allocating the required finances to achieve these within the overall project budget.

Business Intelligence – A range of software applications combined with analytical thinking, used to assess a company's raw data including data mining, reporting and online analytical processing. Core Principle (CP5) of the 7 Core Principles.

CPA – An acronym for 'Cost Per Conversion' or 'Cost Per Acquisition' that refers to a digital advertising pricing model where the company pays for each specified action (e.g. sign up, registration, sale, opt-in).

CPC – An acronym for 'Cost Per Click' or Pay Per Click (PPC) that refers to a digital advertising pricing model whereby the advertiser is charged each time someone clicks on their ad. Google Adwords core Search Network was largely built and is still based on revenues from CPC ads.

CPM – An acronym for 'Cost Per Thousand Impressions' that refers to a digital advertising model whereby the advertiser is charged per 1,000 advertisement impressions on one webpage.

CRM – An acronym for 'Customer Relationship Management' that refers to the management a company's interaction with both current and prospective customers using technology to organize and automate marketing, sales, customer service, and technical support. CRM is Pillar 5 of the 7 Pillars, with a focus on lead nurturing and customer retention through strategies like personalized Email Marketing.

CTA – An acronym for a 'Call to Action' that refers to an instruction to the target market to initiate an immediate response, usually making use of an imperative verb (i.e. "find out more" or "sign up now").

CTC – An acronym for 'Click to Call' that refers to a form of online communication in which a person clicks a button, image or text on a website or search engine results page that initiates a phone call.

Campaign – A coordinated series of actions promoting a product, service or company using a variety of marketing tactics and different mediums, including television, radio, print, online etc.

Cloud (the) – A location where companies and individuals can store digital data online. Physically, this data is housed on multiple servers that are owned and managed by a hosting company (i.e. Dropbox, iCloud).

Cold-Calling – The act of making an unsolicited call by telephone or in person in an attempt to sell goods or services.

Collaborative Consumption – When a group of friends or colleagues watches an event 'together' from separate locations.

Community Marketing – A strategy that engages an audience in an active, non-intrusive prospect and customer conversation, focusing on the needs of existing customers (as opposed to attaining new customers). Akin to Pillar 5 (CRM).

Commercial – A television or radio advertisement.

Conversion Rate – The percentage of users who take a desired action (i.e. the percentage of website visitors who make a purchase).

Competition – Other companies and service providers who are operating in the same markets as you with the same target audience.

Part of Pillar 1. Content

Content – Pillar 1 in both Digital and Traditional Marketing. The promotional assets a company owns and/or creates about their brand, products, services or industry. This covers written copy (i.e. for websites, brochures, blogs, how-to guides), video, audio and visual/imagery.

Content Marketing – The process of creating and distributing valuable and relevant content to attract, acquire, and engage a clearly defined target audience in order to drive customer action which is profitable.

Content Calendars – Editorial calendars that are used to plan and define a company or agency's process of creating and posting content, from idea through to publication.

Content Creators – A person or group of people who coordinate and action the creation of content for a company's content and/or overall marketing and communication strategy.

Cookie Cutter Approach – Approaches that "lack of originality or distinction" and lead to uniform results from the use of a cookie cutter.

Copywriting – The process of producing written online or print content that is used to persuade a target audience or person and increase brand awareness.

Creative Assets – Outputs a company creates and owns as part of the Design function, while taking direction from Branding and utilizing Content. Generally falls under Pillar 2 (UX/Design), but also has a touch of Pillar 1 (Content) and Branding (tP2).

Crowdsourcing – The act of gathering information or input for a particular task or project by enlisting the services of a number of people, either paid or unpaid, generally through the Internet. Generally falls under Pillar 6 (Social Media).

Custom URL – Also known as a 'Vanity URL', a process that condenses your profile URL into a convenient, readable and easily remembered form.

Data – Collected and analyzed facts and statistics that are used to gain insights and inform your Marketing Strategy.

Data Gathering – The process of gathering and measuring information in systematic fashion through a number of mediums.

Design – All forms of Design and User Experience (UX), including but not limited to Web Development, Hosting & Maintenance and Web Design. Design is Pillar 2.

Deliverables – The various outputs, milestones and goals that are achieved and produced by the successful execution of a Marketing Strategy or project.

Digital Marketing – The targeted, measurable, and interactive marketing of products or services using digital platforms and technologies to reach and convert leads into customers.

Direct Marketing – A low cost method of reaching a particular target audience (e.g. Email Marketing, Direct Mail, Telemarketing, Direct Selling, Community Marketing)

Direct Mail – An unsolicited form of advertising sent to prospective customers through paper mail.

Direct Traffic – Traffic that reaches your website though URL's that the visitor has either typed in directly or has reached through their browser bookmarks.

Doer – An action-oriented character who likes to live in Execution Mode (Mode 6). This is the most resourceful Marketing Personality Type (MPT6), one that is not afraid to learn new things and is not satisfied until things are done and done well.

Domain Knowledge – Valid knowledge of an industry or market place and the relevant requirements for a successful marketing strategy within them. Highly relevant to Dimension 6. (Industries) of the 7 Pillars system.

DRTV – An acronym for Direct Response Television that refers to any advertisement on television that persuades the consumers to respond directly, usually either by calling or by visiting a web site. Part of tP7 (Direct Marketing).

Early Bird – A person who arises early in the morning and that arrives early or before others. One who is generally more productive and functions best in mornings.

Earned Media – Also known as 'free media', publicity that is gained through promotional efforts other than advertising. Most common forms include PR, Social Media and organic Search (SEO) Marketing.

EMS – An acronym for 'Email Marketing Solution' that refers to a software service that allows you to build, execute and measure the success of a targeted email marketing campaign (i.e. MailChimp, Campaign Monitor).

Email Marketing – The use of email to serve ads, request business, or solicit sales or donations from your target audience in order to build rapport, trust or brand awareness.

Eras – Different periods of time as in reference to variances in the marketplace landscape (i.e. in terms of technologies available) broken down into Past, Present and Future , or other custom time periods.

Entrepreneur – A person who takes on greater than normal financial risks in order to operate their own business or businesses.

Engagement – Any interaction or action in response to published content from a company or agency as part of a wider marketing strategy (i.e. a 'like', comment or share of a company's promotional Facebook post).

Engagement Rate – A metric used heavily in analyzing the success of a social media campaign or communication. It is the percentage of people who were served the content that directly interacted with it (i.e. like, share, comment).

Event Marketing – Traditional Pillar 6. Any pre-planned, live promotional or educational event, appearance or program. This includes trade shows, conferences, seminars, street fairs, concerts, performances, flash mobs and other forms of guerilla or grass roots marketing.

Event Production – The coordination of a themed activity, display or exhibit (e.g. at a sporting event, music festival or concert) to promote a product, service, cause or company. Part of tP6. Event Marketing.

Facebook – Formed in 2004 by Mark Zuckerberg, Facebook is the most popular social network. It allows you to create profiles, upload photos and video, send messages and keep in touch with your friends, family and colleagues.

Facebook Advertising – Advertising on the social network Facebook which a company or marketing agency pays for. The most popular ad forms are promoted pages and boosted posts (including text, images or videos).

Facebook Page – A public profile specifically created for a business, brand, celebrity, cause and other organization that is 'liked' by a Facebook user in order to keep up to date with the content it posts.

Farmer – Closely related to the Management Angle, Farmers (MPT4) do just that – Manage projects. Good Farmers are generally stable, low key, detail-oriented and risk averse.

Flat Angles – Of the 7 Angles (Dimension 3), flat angles (i.e. Marketing, Creative and Technical) have more marketing specificity, broader career opportunities, generally more tasks and are more conducive to a broader group of people.

Financial Angle – This Sharp Angle belongs to the Number Cruncher (MPT1). Beyond pure finance jobs like an Accountant and Financial Analyst, the Financial skill set helps guide projects and keep them on track, and on budget.

Geo-Targeting – A method of delivering different content to a website visitor based on his or her location (e.g. country, region/ state, city, metro code/zip code, organization, IP address).

Go Vs. No Go Decisions – Decisions which determine whether or not a marketing project, campaign, strategy or initiative will go ahead based on the weighing up and consideration of factors important to the likelihood of success or failure.

Goal Setting – The process of identifying the desired deliverables for your marketing campaign to accomplish and establishing the measurable goals and timeframes required to achieve these.

Google – Both a noun and a verb, Google is the world's most popular search engine with over 67% market share. 'To Google' something (or) means to search for a term on the internet using this search engine. Optimized for in Pillar 3 (Search).

Google+ – A social network from Google which shares some of the features with other popular social networks and microblogging platforms.

Google Adwords – Google's advertising system in which advertisers bid on certain keywords in order for their clickable ads to appear in Google's search results.

Google Algorithm – The formula Google uses to rank the resulting Web pages from a user's search query. Part of Pillar 3 (Search).

Google Analytics – A freemium web analytics service offered by Google that tracks and reports website traffic.

Google Maps – A web-based service that provides detailed information about geographical regions and sites around the world.

Google Keyword Planner – A program that helps you choose relevant keywords plus competitive bids and budgets to use with your campaigns.

GPS – An acronym for 'Global Positioning System' that refers to a radio navigation system that allows land, sea, and airborne users to determine their exact location anywhere in the world.

Grassroots Marketing – Part of tP6 (Event Marketing). A type of marketing that targets communications to a small, specialist group using unconventional or nontraditional methods, with the intention that the group will spread your message to a much larger audience.

Groupthink – The practice of thinking or making decisions as a group in a way that discourages creativity or individual responsibility.

Guerilla Marketing – Also part of tP6 (Event Marketing). Innovative, unconventional, and low-cost marketing techniques aimed at obtaining maximum exposure for a product, service or company.

Hashtag – A word or phrase preceded by a hash or pound sign (#) that is used to identify, categorize and organize messages on social media about a specific topic. Part of Pillar 6 (Social).

Holistic Approach – An approach that involves a company's entire people, processes, products and audience in order to ensure their marketing communications are as well-rounded and effective as possible.

Hosting & Maintenance – The process of providing storage space and access for websites and maintaining the required functionality over a period of time.

Hunter – The Hunter is actually rooted in Sales and reflects a character that is aggressive, proactive and interactive (MPT3). Good hunters know how to go out and engage decision-makers, and convince them to decide in their favor.

Idea Map – A diagram used to visually organize information about how a marketing campaign, strategy or technique is going to function.

Idea Person – Ideal Person (MPT5) is a spark plug and source of creative energy that shines during the early stages of a project, and in the Brainstorming Stage (Mode 1).

Inbound Marketing – A form of marketing that earns the attention of customers, makes companies easily discoverable and draws customers to websites by producing interesting content. Synonymous with Earned Media; includes SEO (Pillar 3), Social Media (Pillar 6) and PR (Traditional Pillar 4).

Incentivizing – Creating initiatives aimed at increasing a consumer's desire to respond positively and act upon a call-to-action (i.e. a special offer, a loyalty program, a discount, a free gift etc.).

Industries – A particular form, branch or sector of economic or commercial activity. Dimension 6 in the 7 Pillars System.

Infomercial(s) – A television program that promotes a product in an informative and supposedly objective way. A mix between tP3 (Advertising) and tP7 (Direct Marketing).

Information Gatherer (IG) – A close relative of Brainstorming and Strategy, the Information Gatherer believes in the power of data (MPT2). They are the fastest and most dynamic web crawlers around, and seem to know how to find information that the rest of us didn't think was possible to locate.

Innovation – CP4 of the Core Principles. The action or process of creatively approaching a problem or creating a solution in a manner which has not yet been previously explored.

In-app Advertising – An ad that is displayed to the user within a mobile phone or tablet application. The offspring of M4 (Online Advertising) and M7 (Mobile).

Instagram – An online mobile photo and video sharing social network that allows you to take pictures and videos to share with you followers. Hybrid of M6 (Social) and M7 (Mobile).

In-store Merchandising – The variety and display of products on sale in a store with the intent to stimulate interest and entices customers to make a purchase. Merchandising is an important part of tP5 (Sales).

Insight(s) – The capacity to gain an accurate and deep intuitive understanding of your target marketing and effectively act on it.

Insite Search – A function that allows you to navigate and search internally through a sites content (e.g. a product search on Amazon). Part of Pillar 3 (Organic Search).

Integrated Marketing (IM) – The application of consistent brand messaging using different promotional methods across both traditional and digital marketing channels. There are 12 Pillars in the Integrated Marketing model.

Internet Marketing – Synonyms: Digital Marketing, Web Marketing, Online Marketing. Advertising and marketing efforts that use the Web and email to drive direct sales via electronic commerce, in addition to sales leads from websites or emails.

Interactive PR – Also known as Online PR, this is the process of using the internet as a medium to communicate messages to the public. Part of Pillar 6 (Social) and a close cousin of tP4 (Public Relations).

Keyword – A particular word or phrase that describes the contents of a Web page relating to a company, product or service. Most relevant in Pillar 3 (Organic Search) and 4 (Online Media).

Keyword Bidding – The process of assigning bid amounts to specific keywords that are used in your target audience's search process. A vital part of Pillar 4 (Media).

Keyword Research – Often used across Pillar 1 (Content), Pillar 3 (Search) and Pillar 4 (Media), this is a practice Digital

Marketing professionals use to find and research actual search terms that people enter into search engines.

Keyword List – A list of words related to a company, product or service that you want to be visible for when your target audience searches online. This can be used for both Search Engine Optimization and digital advertising as part of Pillar 3 (Search) and Pillar 4 (Media).

Knowledge Sharing – Core Principle 6 (Knowledge Sharing) is the activity through which knowledge (information, skills, or expertise) is exchanged among the different members of a marketing team. Often used in M1 (Brainstorming).

KPIs – An acronym for 'Key Performance Indicators' that refers to metrics that are used to evaluate factors that are crucial to the success of a marketing project or campaign. These are commonly set during M3 (Strategy), evaluated in M7 (Analytics) and are related to Core Principle 2 (Goal Driven).

Lead Generation – The process of developing and gaining new consumer interest or inquiries into products or services of a company in order to turn them into successful conversions. This is often the end of objective of the activities carried out under such Pillars as dP4 (Media) and dP6 (Social).

Lead Interaction – The process of communicating and nurturing current and potential future leads. This is a core concept within Pillar 5 (CRM).

Link-Building – The process and SEO technique of acquiring hyperlinks from other websites to your own in order to increase your page's authority ranking in Google. Part of Pillar 3 (Search).

LinkedIn – A social networking site designed specifically for business professionals and the business community. This is used by both individuals and companies under Pillar 6 (Social).

LinkedIn Group – Part of Pillar 6 (Social), this is an online forum set up by an existing LinkedIn users which others can also join to partake in discussion or make new connections. Here users can engage in Core Principle 6 (Active Knowledge Sharing).

Localized Content – Content written specifically for a geographic area and locality. This is part of Pillar 1 (Content) and used in conjunction with a local search strategy within Pillar 3 (Search).

Local SEO – Local Search Engine Optimization is part of Pillar 3 (Search) and refers to specialized digital marketing that increases the visibility of businesses in search rankings for geographically related keywords.

Local Search – Searches against a structured database of local business listings determined through geographic segmentation of a target audience. Part of Pillar 3 (Search).

Location-based Promotions – Promotions that use geo-targeting to serve promotions to a target audience, most commonly within Pillar 6 (Social).

Mailchimp – MailChimp is a freemium web-based application and email marketing service provider that allows companies to execute and measure email marketing campaigns. This is an important tool used within Pillar 5 (CRM) to communicate with either prospective or existing customers.

Markets – Dimension V (Markets) includes all of the local and global exchanges which can be segmented geographically (i.e. Continent, Country, City or State) and demographically (i.e. Income Level, Gender, Age, Ethnicity and other classifications).

Marketing Channels – The set of marketing practices or activities necessary to transfer the ownership of goods from the point of production to the point of consumption. These are decided upon under Mode 3 (Strategy).

Market Research – The process of gathering, analyzing and interpreting information about a market in order to make informed and optimal decisions to shape an effective Marketing Strategy. This is an intersection of Brainstorming (Mode 1), Strategy (Mode 3), Business Intelligence (Core Principle 5) and Research (Angle 4) and is usually carried out by MPT2 (Information Gatherer).

Media – Pillar 4 (Media) comprises all forms of Online Advertising, essentially any paid media placement including banner ads, PPC ads (Pay Per Click), endorsements, sponsored emails and Social Media advertising.

Media Fees – The cost associated with promotional activity carried out through paid forms of Media, Pillar 4.

Mobile App – A computer program designed to run on mobile devices such as smartphones and tablet computers. Part of Pillar 7 (Mobile).

Mobile Device – A portable computing device such as a smartphone or tablet computer that connects to the internet, either through WiFi or cellular data. This is a part of Pillar 7 (Mobile).

Mobile Advertising – Any form of advertising executed through mobile (wireless) phones or other mobile devices such as tablets. A hybrid of both Pillar 4 (Media) and PIllar 7 (Mobile).

Mobile Marketing – Pillar 7 (Mobile) encompasses promotional activity designed for delivery to cell phones, smart phones and tablets, usually as a component of a multi-channel campaign.

Mobile Web – The use of the Internet through handheld mobile devices including Smartphones and Tablets. A part of Pillar 7 (Mobile).

Multivariate – Testing involving two or more variable quantities.

Newsletter – A bulletin issued periodically to the members of a society, business, or organization. This can also be used for promotional purposes by businesses under Traditional Pillar 7 (Direct Marketing).

Night Owl – A person who is habitually active or wakeful at night.

'Nice To Have' Features – Features of an app, website, campaign or project which may not be essential but could increase it's effectiveness. Marketers may have to forgo the inclusion of these attributes if they face constraints, either financial or time based. Usually outlined from Mode 1 (Brainstorming) and decided upon in Mode 3 (Strategy).

Number Cruncher – A close relative of ROI and Finance, the Number Cruncher sees the business world through the lens of Excel spreadsheets (MPT1). A close relative of ROI (Mode 2) and Financial (Angle 6).

Off-page SEO – A key part of Pillar 3 (Search), this covers techniques that can be used to improve the position of a web site in the search engine results page from external sources (e.g. link building).

Online Marketing – Synonyms: Web Marketing, Internet Marketing and Digital Marketing. Advertising and marketing efforts that use the internet and email to drive direct sales via ecommerce and raise brand awareness.

Online Advertising – A form of digital advertising which uses the Internet to deliver promotional marketing messages to consumers through Social Media, search engines or web pages. A subset of Pillar 4 (Media).

Online Publications – Media publications that deliver content to their audiences either primarily or solely online. These fall under Pillar 1 (Content) and well-known examples include the Huffington Post and Buzzfeed.

On-page SEO – A key part of Pillar 3 (Search), this includes factors that have an effect on your Web site or Web page listing in natural search results which you have direct control over (e.g. inclusion of keywords, optimal page titles and image alt tags etc.).

OOH Advertising – An acronym for Out-Of-Home advertising that refers to any form of advertising that reaches the consumer while they are outside the home (e.g. billboards). A component of Traditional Pillar 3 (Advertising).

Original Photography – Copyrighted Images that are commissioned by a company themselves, that are a part of [dP1] Content and also Traditional Pillar 1 (Content).

Organic Reach – The total number of unique people who are shown content through unpaid distribution. A subset of Pillar 6 (Social).

Organic Search – A part of Pillar 3 (Search), this covers listings on search engine results pages that appear because of their relevance to the search terms, as opposed to them being advertisements.

Organic Workflow – Core Principle 7 (Organic & Agile Workflow) is a system that encourages adaptive adjustments to maximize productivity. High performers in Marketing accommodate variations in work styles (Structure vs. Flexibility; Right vs. Left Brain synergy).

Owned Media – The marketing assets or channels that a company controls and is able to utilize in order to direct a chosen set of marketing messages to an audience. Media giants develop such assets under Angle 7 (Venture).

Paid Media – Any form of traditional or paid advertising that you pay for including print, television, radio, paid search, retail/channel. A key aspect of Pillar 4 (Media).

Photoshop – (noun) An image editing software suite created by Adobe and (verb) 'to photoshop' something means to use this software to edit an image. Often used within PIllar 1 (Content) to create imagery for advertising.

Pinterest – A social curation website for sharing and categorizing images found online. Part of Pillar 6 (Social).

PLPs – A "preferred landing page" is a particular page on your website that you would like a particular keyword to rank for. This is used within Pillar 3 (Search).

Podcast – An on-demand digital audio file that is made available to an online audience and can be downloaded to a computer or portable media player. It is typically available as a automatic series of new installments to subscribers and falls under Pillar 1 (Content).

Power User – An expert user of a digital platform who has reached advanced level status in their peers' eyes (for example a top contributor to a forum, a respected member of an online community). This is related to Core Principle 6 (Active Knowledge Sharing).

POS – An acronym for a 'Point of Sale' that refers to the location at which goods are retailed. A subset of Traditional Pillar 5 (Sales).

PPC – An acronym for for 'Pay Per Click' that refers to a business model whereby a company advertises on a website and pays a sum of money to the host website when a user clicks on to the advertisement. A primary component of Pillar 4 (Media).

Product Design – The process of creating a new product to be sold by a business to its customers.

Productivity Apps – Any program or application on a smartphone or tablet device, used to optimize a person's productivity. For example, through time tracking, task scheduling and the setting of reminders. This is a part of Pillar 7 (Mobile) and falls within Core Principle 1 (Time Mastery).

PR – Traditional Pillar 4 (PR) is the management of unpaid, strategic communications between an entity and its target market(s) or the public at large.

Press Conference – An interview given to journalists by a prominent person in order to make an announcement or answer questions. An activity carried out under Traditional Pillar 4 (PR).

Press Release – An official statement issued to newspapers giving information on a particular matter. Part of Traditional Pillar 4 (PR).

Pyramids of Knowledge – The Pyramids of Knowledge are created by crossing the 3rd and 4th Dimensions (Angles and Levels). Pyramids generally have seven different positions and sizes, which represent who is being evaluated on what domain of knowledge.

Qualitative Research – Exploratory, non-numerical research that is used to gain an understanding of underlying reasons, opinions, and motivations within a marketplace. This is a classification of Market Research that occurs within Brainstorming (Mode 1), Strategy (Mode 3), Business Intelligence (Core Principle 5) and Research (Angle 4) and is usually carried out by MPT2 (Information Gatherer).

Quantitative Research – A formal, objective, systematic process in which numerical data are used to obtain information about markets. This type of Market Research occurs within Brainstorming (Mode 1), Strategy (Mode 3), Business Intelligence (Core Principle 5) and Research (Angle 4) and is executed by MPT2 (Information Gatherer).

Recruiting – The act of searching for and hiring optimal people for your company, project and/or team. This relates to Mode 4 (People).

Referrals – New business or customers that have been gained based on currently satisfied customers recommending your product or services to another customer. In Digital Marketing, these are a KPI of Pillar 6 (Social).

Responsive Design – An approach to web page creation that uses flexible layouts and images and cascading style sheet media queries. Responsive design is a principle of Pillar 2 (Design) and the goal is to build web pages that detect the visitor's screen size and orientation and change the layout accordingly.

Retention – A core aspect of Pillar 5 (CRM), the retention of customers refers to keeping your repeat business from clients secure and on-going.

Revenue Estimates – The project cash flow for a company, project or campaign over a defined period of time in the future. This can be used as a decision making tool in order to determine how viable an investment or the profitability of a project might be. A part of Mode 2 (ROI).

ROI – Closely related to the Angle 5 (Financial), Mode 2 (ROI) is where a Marketing team locks-in its forward-looking goals and associated budgets.

Sales – Traditional Pillar 5 (Sales), is a close cousin of [dP5] CRM and is focused on customer development and management. It includes in-store merchandising, Point of Sale (POS) strategy and is closely related to Traditional Pillar 2 (Branding).

SaaS – An acronym for 'Software as a Service' that refers to a software licensing and delivery model in which software is licensed on a subscription basis and is centrally hosted. It is related to Mode 5 (Tools).

Search – Pillar 3 (Search) corresponds to the principles of Search all over the web including search engines, insite search, product search and the search for anything within specific niche sites.

Search Engines – A program that searches for and identifies items in a database that correspond to keywords or characters specified by the user, used especially for finding particular sites on the internet. A core component of Pillar 3 (Search).

Segmentation – To divide the marketplace into segments geographically, demographically, psychographically or behaviorally. This is related to Dimension 5 (Markets) and Pillar 5 (CRM).

Seminars – A conference or other meeting for discussion or training. These fall under Traditional Pillar 6 (Event Marketing).

SEO – An acronym for 'Search Engine Optimization' that refers to the process of maximizing the number of visitors to a particular website by ensuring that the site appears high on the list of results returned by a search engine. A primary component of Pillar 3 (Search).

SERP – An acronym for 'Search Engine Results Page' that refers to the listing of results returned by a search engine in response to a keyword query. This is related to Pillar 3 (Search).

Sharp Angle – Part of Dimension 4 (Angles), these are critical components with more specialized skill sets that help to shape and organize the Pillars, and consequently, the Universe of Marketing.

Signifier (of a company) – A key component of a company's marketing and branding strategy that clearly differentiates them from it's competitors (e.g. the content they produce and publish). This is related to [dP1] Content, Traditional Pillar 1 (Content) and Traditional Pillar 2 (Branding).

Snapchat – A mobile app that allows users to send and receive "self-destructing" photos and videos. Photos and videos taken with the app are called Snaps. This is a part of Pillar 6 (Social).

Social Media – Pillar 6 (Social) includes all forms of organic Social Media activity. This includes communications within all social networks, relationship building with prospective customers and industry influencers, as well as content distribution.

Social Networks – A dedicated website or other application that enables users to communicate with each other by posting information, comments, messages, images, etc. A core area of Pillar 6 (Social).

Spam – Irrelevant or inappropriate messages sent on the Internet to a large number of recipients.

Sponsorship – A form marketing in which a company pays a fee to have their brand associated with an event or cause in order to gain recognition. Closely related to Traditional Pillar 3 (Advertising) and Traditional Pillar 6 (Event Marketing).

Staff Training – The process of providing your staff with structured programs in order to improve their skills and increase work performance. This falls under Mode 4 (People).

Stakeholders – A person with an interest or concern in a business, related to Mode 4 (People).

Stock Photography – A component of Pillar 1 (Content), this refers to photographs by a third party that are licensed for promotional and commercial use by a company.

Storyboard – A sequence of drawings, typically with some directions and dialogue, representing the shots or screens planned for a future campaign, app or advertisement. Used during Mode 1 (Brainstorming).

Strategy – Mode 3 (Strategy) entails the creation and articulation of a marketing plan (utilizing 1 or more Pillars), based on all of the information provided and discovered through the other Modes.

Strategic Planning – An organization's process of defining its strategy, or direction, and making decisions on allocating its resources to pursue this strategy. A component of Mode 3 (Strategy).

Streaming – A method of transmitting or receiving video and audio material data over a computer network as a steady, continuous flow, allowing playback to proceed while subsequent data is being received.

Tagline – A catchphrase or slogan used primarily in Pillar 1 (Content), Traditional Pillar 2 (Branding) and Traditional Pillar 3 (Advertising).

Telemarketing – A form of marketing that solicits potential customers to services and products over the phone and a core aspect of Traditional Pillar 7 (Direct Marketing).

Time Management – The ability to use one's time effectively or productively, especially at work. A core component of Core Principle 1 (Time Mastery).

Traditional Marketing – Think Mad Men. This is captured in the 7 Pillars of Traditional Marketing and covers the channels utilized before the dawn of the digital marketing age, such as print advertisements, newsletters, billboards, flyers and newspaper print ads.

Trade Shows – An exhibition organized so that companies in a specific industry can showcase and demonstrate their latest products, service, study activities of rivals and examine recent market trends and opportunities. These are a key aspect of Traditional Pillar 6 (Event Marketing).

Traffic Estimates – Forecasts of the amount of traffic you may get to your website for the use of a particular keyword. This relates to Mode 2 (ROI) and PIllar 3 (Search).

Transferable Skills – Skills developed in one situation by employees that can be transferred to another situation. This is related to Mode 4 (People).

Twitter – A social networking platform that allows users to post images, videos and microblogs up to a character limit of 140 characters. This falls under Pillar 6 (Social).

Tweet – A posting made on the social media website Twitter, related to Pillar 6 (Social).

UX – Pillar 2 (Design) covers all aspects of digital UX, including Web Development, App Development, Web Design and even Web Hosting & Maintenance. Every element on every page of a website calls for well thought-out UX, including creative assets, like banner ads, forms, calls to action and header graphics.

USP – An acronym for 'Unique Selling Proposition/Point' that refers to a factor that differentiates a product from its competitors, such as the lowest cost, the highest quality or the first-ever product of its kind. This can be communicated through Pillar 1 (Content) and Traditional Pillar 2 (Branding).

URL – The generic term for all types of names and addresses that refer to objects on the World Wide Web.

Vanity URL – A unique web address that is branded for marketing purposes optimized to be easy to remember, usable and sharable. This can be used as part of Pillar 2 (Design) to give the customer a better User Experience (UX) when searching for the company/product online.

Video Assets – The video content owned by a company for digital usage on their website or social media channels. A core part of Pillar 1 (Content).

Visionary – The most evolved of all MPTs (MPT7). Their clear-sighted comprehension of particular business problems and optimal solutions, when matched by an ability to articulate that vision, yields unparalleled potential.

Website – A company's website is a set of related web pages on an internet domain that they own. How effective this is at achieving the goals they set for it is shaped by their effective use of Pillar 1 (Content) and Pillar 2 (Design).

Website Copy – The written content that is created for a company's website and is a subset of Pillar 1 (Content).

Web Design – The many different skills and disciplines in the production, design and maintenance of websites. A core principle within Pillar 2 (Design).

Web Development – A term used to describe the work involved in developing a web site for the Internet or an intranet (a private network). This activity is related to Pillar 2 (Design).

Website Header Graphic – Also known as a hero image, this is a large banner image, prominently placed on a web page, generally in the front and center and is an aspect of Pillar 2 (Design).

Webinar(s) – A seminar conducted over the Internet that falls under Traditional Pillar 6 (Event Marketing). These are often promoted online via Pillar 6 (Social).

Web Page – A single, hypertext document on the World Wide Web that can incorporate text, graphics, sounds and video. This is created in Pillar 2 (Design).

Wireframing – An important step in any screen design process as part of Pillar 2 (Design). It allows a designer to define the information hierarchy of their design, making it easier to plan the layout according to how they want the user to process the information.

WordPress – A free and open-source content management system (CMS) for managing a website's content based on PHP and MySQL. Corresponds to Pillar 1 (Content) and Pillar 2 (Design).

World Wide Web – An information system on the Internet that allows documents to be connected to other documents by hypertext links, enabling the user to search for information by moving from one document to another.

White Belt – A White Belt is very new to the marketing world, and although they may be smart people, their digital IQ, for whatever reason, has not yet been developed. This falls under Dimension 4 (The 7 Levels).

www.ingramcontent.com/pod-product-compliance
Lightning Source LLC
LaVergne TN
LVHW021500080426
835509LV00018B/2357